Traudl Hoops / Wiklef Hoops

Stundenblätter
»Julius Caesar«

W0066445

39 Seiten Beilage

Ernst Klett Verlag

Reihe: Stundenblätter Englisch

Als Textausgabe wird
The Alexander Shakespeare „Julius Caesar"
(Klettbuch 57612) zugrunde gelegt.

CIP-Titelaufnahme der Deutschen Bibliothek

Hoops, Traudl:
Stundenblätter „Julius Caesar" / Traudl Hoops; Wiklef Hoops.
1. Aufl. – Stuttgart: Klett, 1988
& Beil.
(Reihe Stundenblätter Englisch)
  ISBN 3-12-925142-1

NE: Hoops, Wiklef:

ISBN 3-12-925142-1

1. Auflage 1988
Alle Rechte vorbehalten
Fotomechanische Wiedergabe nur mit Genehmigung des Verlags
© Ernst Klett Verlage GmbH u. Co. KG, Stuttgart 1988
Satz: G. Müller, Heilbronn; W. Röck, Weinsberg
Druck: W. Röck, Weinsberg
Einbandgestaltung: Zembsch' Werkstatt, München

Inhalt

Zu Konzeption und Aufbau der Unterrichtssequenz

Shakespeare ist schwer

„Die Shakespeare-Stunde muß zu einer Stunde des Genusses für die Schüler werden, in der ihre Seelen aufgehen in der Gedankenwelt des größten Menschen- und Seelenkenners aller Zeiten, in der sie erst unbestimmt fühlen und dann sich zu immer größerer Klarheit darüber durchringen, daß ihnen aus des Dichters Werken nicht nur eine vergangene Welt entgegenblickt, die unserer Zeit der modernen Sachlichkeit nichts mehr zu sagen hätte, sondern daß sie Gedanken darin finden, die höchst modern sind, weil sie ewig sind."[1]

Das Zitat könnte von Brutus stammen. In unserer heutigen prosaischeren Zeit und gewitzt durch die Lektüre von „Julius Caesar" (von nun an als JC abgekürzt) – dem Drama, in dem der Idealist moralischer Sieger bleibt, die Realisten aber seine Grabrede halten – sollten wir vielleicht unsere Forderungen bescheidener formulieren: Es muß alles getan werden, daß die Schüler angesichts der großen Schwierigkeit, die die Lektüre eines Shakespeare-Dramas für sie bedeutet, nicht völlig „dem Frust anheimfallen", sondern wenigstens ansatzweise verstehen, warum Shakespeare auch heute noch als einer der größten Autoren der Weltliteratur gilt. Demgemäß haben wir die Konzeption der vorliegenden Unterrichtssequenz nicht daran ausgerichtet, was wünschenswert wäre, sondern was wir für realisierbar halten. Diese Entscheidung führt unter anderem zu dem für viele „gestandene" Anglisten sicher schmerzhaften Verzicht auf einen Großteil der Shakespeare-Philologie. Aber uns erscheint es wichtiger, daß die Schüler interessiert mitarbeiten und Shakespeare in guter Erinnerung behalten, als daß sie den Unterschied zwischen Quartos und Folios, die Feinheiten der Shakespeare-Editionstechnik oder verschiedene Formen des „pun" eher widerwillig memoriert haben.

Warum JC?

Weil Shakespeare-Dramen für Schüler schwierig sind, hat sich die Praxis herausgebildet, ein möglichst kurzes Shakespeare-Drama zu behandeln – JC und „Macbeth" sind so zu den beiden am häufigsten im Englischunterricht behandelten Dramen avanciert. Man mag diese enge Kanonbildung bedauern, aber sie ist didaktisch durchaus plausibel.

JC zeichnet sich gegenüber „Macbeth" in didaktischer Hinsicht vor allem durch folgende Eigenschaften[2] aus:
- relativ einfaches Vokabular
- relativ wenig sprachliche Bilder
- klarer Handlungsaufbau
- wenig zeitgenössische Anspielungen.

Wieviel Hintergrund?

Die Schüler sollten auf jeden Fall einen Überblick über die Vielfalt von Shakespeares Werk erhalten (vgl. die 1. Stunde), auch wenn dieses Wissen für die vorliegende Unterrichtssequenz nicht unmittelbar erforderlich ist, da eine ernstgemeinte „Einordnung von JC in Shakespeares Werk" nur dann möglich ist, wenn die Schüler auch andere Dramen Shakespeares kennen. Ein möglicher Schritt in diese Richtung wird in der 1. Zusatzstunde zur 10. Stunde skizziert.

Ebenso selbstverständlich ist eine kurze

Einführung in das elisabethanische Englisch (vgl. 2. Stunde). Schließlich erwarten wir, daß sich die Schüler ernsthaft mit dem Originaltext auseinandersetzen. Allerdings sollte das elisabethanische Englisch nicht zum Selbstzweck werden – die Schüler haben genügend Schwierigkeiten mit modernem Englisch!

Auch wenn in unserem Unterrichtsvorschlag die theatralische Umsetzung des Dramentextes wegen des damit verbundenen großen Zeitaufwandes nicht einbezogen ist, sollten die Schüler wenigstens eine grobe Vorstellung von der gesellschaftlichen Bedeutung und den Aufführungsgegebenheiten des elisabethanischen Theaters vermittelt bekommen (vgl. 3./4. Stunde). Die Schüler erhalten so einen Einblick in eine Zeit, in der Theater noch nicht, wie heute oft, abgehobene und anstrengende „Kunst", sondern auch entspannende Unterhaltung „fürs Volk" war. Auch Shakespeare war in seiner Zeit nicht mehr als „ein Erfolgsautor des kommerziellen Unterhaltungstheaters, bewundert wegen der Leichtigkeit, mit der er eingängige und zugkräftige Stücke schrieb und Leute der verschiedensten Schichten und Interessen anlockte".[3]

Auf eine Behandlung des „elisabethanischen Weltbildes" haben wir verzichtet, da die neuere Shakespeare-Forschung gezeigt hat, daß sowohl das Weltbild der damaligen Zeit als auch Shakespeares Auseinandersetzung mit ihm wesentlich komplexer und vielschichtiger waren, als dies Tillyards – einstmals berühmten – Pauschalierungen vermuten lassen. Dem folgenden einleuchtenden Vorschlag von Habicht sind wir nur deshalb nicht gefolgt, weil er uns für die Unterrichtspraxis zu aufwendig erscheint: „Inhaltlich sollten historische Bezugspunkte nicht in nochmaliger Verdünnung der Tillyardschen Weltbildpauschalitäten angeboten werden; angemessener schiene es, die in den dramatischen Situationen selbst zugespitzten Probleme und Widersprüche durch ein Text- und Bildmaterial zu präzisieren, das vom Spektrum elisabethanischer Wirklichkeit einen Begriff vermittelt."[4]

Lesedrama oder „drama in performance"?

Aus gattungstheoretischer Sicht ist diese Frage sicher falsch gestellt, vor allem in bezug auf Shakespeares Dramen. Trotzdem bleiben der Text und ein angemessenes Verständnis desselben Basis- und Ausgangspunkt jeglicher weitergehenden, auf die theatralische Realisierung zielenden Betrachtung des Dramas: „Dabei ist die theatralische Gesamtwirkung das von einem theaternahen Autor wie Shakespeare recht eigentlich Intendierte. Das aber heißt, daß, will man nicht nur die Erscheinungsbilder der Shakespeare-Rezeption im Wandel der Zeit studieren, als objektive Richtschnur eben doch die Frage nach Shakespeares Intentionen zu stellen ist. [...] Shakespeares Intentionen begreifen die Theatralik und den Publikumsbezug ein; *für deren Erschließung indes haben wir nur die Texte und die Struktur der Dramen selbst als primäre Grundlage.* Auf die Texte sehen wir uns also verwiesen, mit der durchaus kommunikativen Erkenntnis freilich, daß diese gleichsam als ein System von Signalen aufzufassen sind, das über sich hinausweist und konkrete Aufführungserlebnisse anzustoßen vermag."[5]

Eine sorgfältige Erarbeitung des Textes wird damit zur „Pflicht"-Übung – eine Behandlung von JC als „drama in performance", wie von Busacker (vgl. unsere Literaturhinweise) vorgeschlagen, kann als zusätzliche, allerdings sehr zeitaufwendige „Kür"-Übung betrachtet werden, die angesichts der sprachlichen Schwierigkeiten des Textes vielleicht doch eher einem anderen Beispieldrama im Rahmen des Deutschunterrichts überlassen werden sollte. Wem die hier vorgeschlagenen „Pflichtfiguren" nicht ausreichen, sei auf die zahlreichen Anregungen und Vorschläge zur Behandlung von JC als „drama in performance" bei Busacker verwiesen.

Medien zu JC

Es gibt eine vieldiskutierte und mit vielen Stars (Marlon Brando als Antony, James Mason als Brutus und John Gielgud als Cassius) besetzte amerikanische Verfilmung von JC (Regie: Joseph L. Mankiewicz) aus dem Jahr 1953 (vgl. dazu ausführlich Busacker, S. 217–238), die allerdings weit über 100,– DM kostet und über die Cinema International Corporation (16-mm-Abteilung), Kaiserstr. 66, 6000 Frankfurt/Main, bezogen werden kann. Wesentlich kürzer (ca. 20 Minuten) und leichter zu beschaffen (über den British Council) ist der Unterrichtsfilm "JC by William Shakespeare. An Introduction. Educational Limited... New Shakespeare Series 1968". Obwohl dieser Film in vieler Hinsicht problematisch ist, kann er trotzdem als optische Folie im Unterricht gute Dienste leisten.
In unserem Unterrichtsvorschlag haben wir nur gelegentlich den Einsatz einer Tonkassette (Soundtrack des Mankiewicz-Filmes) vorgesehen, die über den British Council bezogen werden kann.

Zur Interpretation von JC

Jeder konkrete Unterrichtsvorschlag zu einem literarischen Text basiert notwendigerweise auf einem *bestimmten* Verständnis des Textes, das man offenlegen sollte. Wir haben uns wesentlich an M. E. Hartsock (s. Literaturhinweise) orientiert,

die JC als ausgesprochen „ambiguous play" versteht: "It is the contention of this paper that the ambiguities of JC cannot be resolved and that Shakespeare's use of his sources shows that he did not intend for them to be resolved." (S. 58)
Allerdings stimmen wir der folgenden These der Autorin nicht ganz zu, weil sie nach unserer Meinung eine zu moderne Sichtweise an Shakespeare heranträgt: "It is more convincing to say that JC ist not a problem play but a play about a problem: the difficulty – perhaps the impossibility – of knowing the truth of men and history." (S. 61)
Wer die Thesen von Hartsock im Unterricht prüfen möchte, findet ausführliche Zitate aus den Quellen in der Arden Edition.

Zur Textausgabe

Sämtliche Zitatbelege beziehen sich auf die von H. L. Kennedy im Rahmen des „Alexander Shakespeare" herausgegebene Ausgabe von JC, die in Deutschland vom Klett-Verlag angeboten wird und weitgehend mit der Zeilenzählung der Arden Edition übereinstimmt. Diese Ausgabe ist sehr ausführlich kommentiert und enthält darüber hinaus eine Einführung in das elisabethanische Zeitalter, in die Sprache, die Figuren und den „plot" des Stückes. Am Anfang jeder Szene wird eine kurze Inhaltsangabe gegeben. Die Ausgabe wird abgerundet durch eine an Figuren und Themen orientierte Gesamtinterpretation des Dramas („Summing up") und einen Themen- und Motivindex. Die Inhaltsangaben zu den einzelnen Szenen haben den Vorteil, daß sich die Schüler eine Szene schnell vergegenwärtigen können. Andererseits werden sie auf jeden Fall durch die Hausaufgaben und die für den Unterricht vorgeschlagenen Fragen und Arbeitsaufträge dazu gebracht,

7

sich ausführlich mit konkreten Textstellen auseinanderzusetzen.

Zum Aufbau der Unterrichtssequenz

Die Schüler sollten das Drama unter Zuhilfenahme einer deutschen Übersetzung gelesen haben, bevor in der 5. Stunde mit der konkreten Behandlung des Dramentextes selbst begonnen wird.

Zunächst wird in der 5. Stunde eine Handlungsübersicht erarbeitet, damit die Schüler einen geordneten Überblick über das gesamte Drama haben. Die Behandlung des Textes in den folgenden 11 Stunden (6.–16. Stunde) folgt im wesentlichen der Chronologie der Dramenhandlung und stützt sich weitgehend auf die detaillierte Analyse ausgewählter Textstellen.

Der Einstieg in die konkrete Textarbeit erfolgt in der 6. Stunde mit einer Analyse von I.2 (Cassius versucht, Brutus zur Teilnahme an der Verschwörung zu überreden). Hierbei stehen vor allem Fragen des persuasiven Sprachgebrauchs im Mittelpunkt. (Diese Fragestellung wird dann, im Hinblick auf den Bereich der „öffentlichen" Rhetorik, bei der Analyse der Forumsreden in der 13./14. Stunde wiederaufgenommen.) In der 7.–9. Stunde stehen die drei Hauptfiguren des Dramas im Mittelpunkt. (Die vierte Hauptfigur, Antonius, wird in der 12. Stunde ausführlich behandelt.)

Die anschließenden Analysen von Brutus' Monologen (10. Stunde) und seiner Rede vor den Verschwörern (11. Stunde) zeigen, daß Brutus keineswegs eine eindimensionale Idealfigur ist, wie es zunächst den Anschein hat. Diese Infragestellung von Brutus' moralischer Integrität wird weiter vorangetrieben durch Antonius' Eintritt in die Dramenhandlung (12. Stunde). Obwohl Antonius selbst ein mora-

lisch zweifelhafter Charakter ist, ist er die einzige Figur, die Brutus' moralische Qualitäten ernsthaft in Frage stellt.

Auch die Forumsreden (13./14. Stunde) sind von dem Gegensatz dieser beiden Figuren bestimmt; allerdings steht hier nicht mehr Brutus' moralische Integrität in Frage, sondern die mangelnde öffentliche Durchsetzungskraft einer ausschließlich moralischen Position.

Der nach den Forumsreden im Grunde schon besiegelte Untergang der Verschwörer wird in der 15. und 16. Stunde betrachtet: Die Gegenüberstellung der beiden Parteien im 4. Akt unterstreicht die Tragik einer rein idealistischen Position. Gleichzeitig läßt die Extremsituation neue Seiten der beiden Verschwörer sichtbar werden.

In den letzten beiden Stunden wird das Drama in seiner Gesamtheit betrachtet: In der 17. Stunde durch die genauere Betrachtung eines Motivs (Vorzeichen), in der 18. Stunde durch die Gegenüberstellung dreier Interpretationsthesen für eine Gesamtdeutung des Dramas. Diese Thesen werden dabei nicht als sich ausschließende Alternativen, sondern als unterschiedliche, sich ergänzende Hinsichten auf das Drama verstanden.

Anmerkungen

1 Draber, M.: Ein Beitrag zur Methodik des Shakespeare-Unterrichts. *Neuphil. Monatsschrift* 3 (1932), S. 205.

2 Vgl. dazu ausführlich Busacker (vgl. unsere Literaturhinweise), S. 33 ff.

3 Suerbaum, Ulrich: Shakespeare – Zu schwierig? *a & e* 6 (1980), S. 159–169, hier S. 159.

4 Habicht, Werner: Zum Shakespeare-Bild heute – Tendenzen und Impulse neuerer Shakespeare-Forschung. *a & e* 3 (1977), S. 39–52, hier S. 49.

5 Habicht, a.a.O., S. 43.

Literaturhinweise

In den folgenden Literaturhinweisen werden nur einige wenige Titel kurz charakterisiert, die uns als besonders hilfreich für die unterrichtliche Vorbereitung des Lehrers erscheinen. Ausführliche bibliographische Hinweise zu JC enthalten die unten aufgeführten Arbeiten von Busacker und Häublein/Wenig.

Zu Shakespeare allgemein

Schabert, Ina (Hg.): *Shakespeare-Handbuch. Die Zeit – Der Mensch – Das Werk – Die Nachwelt.* Stuttgart: Kröner 1978.
Ein umfassendes Standardwerk, das fast keine Frage zu Shakespeare und seiner Zeit unbeantwortet läßt. Sehr umfangreiche bibliographische Hinweise.

Müller-Schwefe, Gerhard: *William Shakespeare. Welt – Werk – Wirkung.* Berlin/New York: de Gruyter 1978.
Eine kompakte, nach Gattungen gegliederte Darstellung von Shakespeares Werk, mit besonderer Berücksichtigung medialer (Shakespeares Dramen als „Partituren" für Theateraufführungen und Verfilmungen) sowie rezeptions- und wirkungsgeschichtlicher Fragen. Zahlreiche bibliographische Hinweise.

Suerbaum, Ulrich: *Shakespeares Dramen.* Düsseldorf/Bern/München: Bagel/Francke 1980 (= Studienreihe Englisch Bd. 25).
Keine traditionelle Darstellung von Shakespeares Werk, sondern eine problemorientierte Einführung in die Beschäftigung mit Shakespeare (1. Probleme, 2. Die historischen Bedingungen, 3. Dramaturgie, 4. Gattungen). Zwischenüberschriften wie „Wie komplexe Figuren gemacht werden" signalisieren, daß Wissenschaft, im Gegensatz zu gängigen deutschen Vorstellungen und deutscher Praxis, auch ohne Krawatte und ehrfürchtigen Gesichtsausdruck betrieben werden kann. Ausgewählte kommentierte Literaturhinweise und bibliographischer Anhang.

Ahrens, Rüdiger (Hg.): *William Shakespeare. Didaktisches Handbuch.* 3 Bde. München: Fink 1982.
Eine etwas additiv strukturierte Sammlung von Aufsätzen zur Behandlung von Shakespeare im Unterricht. Enthält in Band 2 zwei Aufsätze zu JC:
– Kurt Otten: Politische Rhetorik als kommunikationstheoretisches Problem. Eine Darstellung anhand der Tragödien JC und Coriolanus. Bd. 2, S. 517–559.
– Lothar Bredella: Shakespeares JC im Englischunterricht: Ein hermeneutisches Modell. Bd. 2, S. 561–593.

Zu „Julius Caesar"

Hartsock, Mildred E.: The Complexity of JC. *PMLA* 81 (1966), S. 56–62.
Dieser Aufsatz gibt einen kondensierten Überblick über die wesentlichen Positionen zur Interpretation von JC. Die Autorin selbst vertritt die These, daß JC von Shakespeare bewußt ambig gestaltet worden ist und belegt ihre Ansicht durch einen Vergleich mit den Quellen: Alle Abweichungen Shakespeares haben zu einer größeren Komplexität und Ambiguität der Figuren geführt.

Busacker, Klaus: *Shakespeares JC.* Vorschläge zur Behandlung des Dramas in einem Leistungskurs. Würzburg: Königshausen + Neumann 1982.

Diese umfangreiche und anregende Arbeit stellt das Drama als „play-in-performance" in den Mittelpunkt. Demgemäß konzentrieren sich die Vorschläge auf Fragen der Dramaturgie und Regie und der medialen Rezeption (Verfilmungen, Aufführungsgeschichte). Der gewählte Ansatz ist theoretisch plausibel, aber in der Praxis nur unter unverhältnismäßigem Zeitaufwand (ca. 30 Stunden) realisierbar. Der Band enthält außerdem eine sehr ausführliche Begründung für die Behandlung von JC, ausführlich erläuterte Arbeitsblätter und ein Kapitel zum Einsatz von Übersetzungen und Vorschläge zum Vergleich von JC mit John Bowens Adaptation *Heil Caesar!*. Umfangreiche Bibliographie.

Häublein, Ernst/Wenig, Edelbert: *Shakespeare's JC*. A Teacher's Guide. Berlin: Cornelsen-Velhagen & Klasing 1984.

Ein etwas unübersichtlich präsentierter Vorschlag zur szenenweisen Behandlung des Dramas mit durchaus wissenschaftlichem Anspruch (über 200 Anmerkungen, umfangreiche Bibliographie) in englischer Sprache. Insgesamt wird u. E. eine zu detaillierte Behandlung der einzelnen Szenen vorgeschlagen (z. B. allein 4 Stunden für I/2, vgl. S. 15); zum Teil sind die Vorschläge zu stark mit literaturwissenschaftlicher Terminologie überfrachtet (vgl. die Folie S. 24f. zur rhetorischen Analyse von I.2 oder die Vorschläge zu den Forumsreden S. 68f.).

Übersetzungen

Es gibt zahlreiche Übersetzungen (vgl. dazu Busacker) von JC. Für den Unterricht am besten geeignet erscheint uns die relativ wörtliche, wissenschaftlich zuverlässige Prosaübersetzung von Klose, Dietrich: *JC. Englisch und Deutsch*. Stuttgart: Reclam [2]1983.

Darstellung der Einzelstunden

1. Stunde:
Shakespeares Werk / Hinführung zu „Julius Caesar"

Didaktische Vorbemerkungen

Die Einleitungsstunde hat vor allem zwei Ziele. Zum einen soll sie den Schülern einen groben Überblick über Shakespeares Werk und Leben geben, zum anderen soll sie den Einstieg in das im Mittelpunkt dieser Unterrichtseinheit stehende Drama vorbereiten. Wichtig an Shakespeares Biographie ist in erster Linie, daß den Schülern die große zeitliche Distanz zu Shakespeare bewußt wird.

Die Stunde beginnt mit einer Reihe von Zitaten aus unterschiedlichen Werken Shakespeares, die als „Geflügelte Worte" (Büchmann) Eingang in den deutschen Zitatenschatz gefunden haben (vgl. Worksheet No. 1 auf dem Stundenblatt). Ausgehend von den Zitatquellen wird eine tabellarische Übersicht über Shakespeares Werk (vgl. Worksheet No. 2) besprochen. Dieser Teil der Stunde schließt mit einem Schülerreferat über Shakespeares Biographie (vgl. Zusatztext zur 1. Stunde).

Im zweiten Teil der Stunde wird die häusliche Lektüre von „Julius Caesar" (= JC) durch einen Überblick über die römische Geschichte und Cäsars Rolle in ihr vorbereitet (vgl. Worksheet No. 3). Die Stunde schließt mit der Aufgabenstellung für die häusliche Lektüre des Dramas.

Verlauf der Stunde

1. Unterrichtsschritt: Shakespeares Werk

Der Einstieg erfolgt über eine Auswahl von auch im deutschen Sprachraum bekannten Shakespeare-Zitaten (Quelle: Büchmann). Auf diese Weise erfahren die Schüler, daß sie Shakespeare, sozusagen unbewußt, bereits „kennen" und daß er auch außerhalb Englands ein einflußreicher Autor war. Hinzu kommt, als Motivationshilfe, der Aha-Effekt, wenn das deutsche „Geflügelte Wort" gefunden worden ist. Nebenbei werden so auf spielerische Weise einige Dramentitel eingeführt.

Die Schüler erhalten als Handout die Zitate auf dem Worksheet No. 1. Worksheet samt Übersetzung der Zitate s. Stundenblatt (für die Schülerkopien rechte Seite abdecken). Die Zitate werden im Unterrichtsgespräch übersetzt, und es wird jeweils die Quelle ermittelt (hier muß der Lehrer allerdings in vielen Fällen aushelfen). Gesucht ist nicht so sehr die genaue wörtliche Übersetzung, sondern die sprichwörtliche deutsche Entsprechung. (Das Ganze kann auch als Quiz organisiert werden.)

Der Lehrer schreibt die einzelnen Zitatquellen, nach Gattungen geordnet, an die Tafel. Am Ende werden die Überschriften für die Kolumnen gesucht, dann wird die tabellarische Übersicht (vgl. Worksheet No. 2) ausgeteilt und kurz besprochen (unsichere Chronologie, deshalb nur ungefähre Gruppenbildung; Shakespeares poetry; Subkategorien „romances" und „Roman plays"). Falls die Zitatenliste gekürzt wird, sollten möglichst viele unterschiedliche Dramen als Quellen erhalten bleiben.

11

Shakespeare, William (baptized April 26, 1564, Stratford-on-Avon, Warwickshire – d. April 23, 1616, Stratford-on-Avon), poet and
5 dramatist widely regarded as the greatest writer of all time. His plays, written in the late 16th and early 17th centuries for a small repertory theatre, are today perform-
10 ed more often and in more countries than ever before. Ben Jonson's prophecy that he "was not of an age, but for all time" has been marvellously fulfilled.
15 His early life was spent in Stratford-on-Avon, where he almost certainly attended the local grammar school. At 18 he married a local girl, Anne Hathaway, who bore him a daugh-
20 ter, Susanna, and twins, Hamnet and Judith. By 1584 he had emerged as a rising playwright in London. He continued to live there, enjoying fame and prosperity as a mem-
25 ber of London's leading theatre company, the Lord Chamberlain's Company (afterward known as the King's Men). In about 1610 he retired to his birthplace and lived as a
30 country gentleman. His will was made in March 1616, a few months before his death. He was buried in the parish church at Stratford.

Frontispiece of the First Folio edition, the Droeshout engraving

From Encyclopaedia Britannica Micropaedia

Aus: *Life-Language-Literature*. Stuttgart: Ernst Klett Verlag 1982, S. 220.

Annotations
repertory theatre a theatre in which a permanent acting company stages several productions each season – *Ben Jonson* (1572–1637) actor, author and friend of Shakespeare's – *parish* area with its own church and priest or minister

2. Unterrichtsschritt:
Shakespeares Biographie

Ein Schüler referiert den Zusatztext zur 1. Stunde („William Shakespeare") und schreibt dabei die wichtigsten Daten an die Tafel. Wichtig ist hier die Erkenntnis, daß man eigentlich sehr wenig über Shakespeare weiß und daß die zeitliche Distanz zu seiner Zeit immerhin fast 400 Jahre beträgt. Am Ende dieses Schritts sollte deshalb kurz überlegt werden, welche Rezeptionsprobleme diese große zeitliche Distanz möglicherweise mit sich bringt (Weltbild, historische Situation, Sprache).

3. Unterrichtsschritt:
Der historische Cäsar

Als Hinführung zu JC erhalten die Schüler einen kurzen Überblick über die Geschichte Roms und Cäsars Bedeutung für sie. Die Schüler sollen vor allem erkennen, daß Cäsars Herrschaft praktisch eine fast 500jährige republikanische Tradition beendete und daß von daher die Angst vor einer neuen Diktatur als Motiv für Cäsars Ermordung durchaus realistisch war.
Zunächst wird im Unterrichtsgespräch an der Tafel zusammengetragen, was die Schüler über Rom und Cäsar wissen. Anschließend wird Worksheet No. 3 ausgeteilt und vom Lehrer erläutert. Zum Abschluß wird an Hand der Landkarte gemeinsam ermittelt, welche (heutigen) Länder zu Cäsars Zeit zum Römischen Reich gehörten.

4. Unterrichtsschritt/Hausaufgabe:
Aufgabenstellung für die häusliche Lektüre von JC

Aus den im Abschnitt zur Konzeption der Unterrichtseinheit genannten Gründen wird das Drama von den Schülern zu Hause in einer deutschen Übersetzung gelesen. In Frage kommt hier entweder die Übersetzung von A. W. Schlegel, Reclams Universal-Bibliothek oder die Prosaübersetzung von D. Klose in der zweisprachigen Reclam-Ausgabe, Universal-Bibliothek Nr. 9816/3/.
Zu der Lektüre werden die folgenden beiden Aufgabenstellungen gegeben:
1. Read the drama carefully. Write a short summary of each of the five acts and find an adequate headline for each act. The summary should describe the function of the individual act as regards the total action of the play.
2. Analyze the function(s) of the first scene.

Hausaufgabe

Die Schüler erhalten Worksheet No. 1 und 2 zur 2. Stunde für die Vorbereitung auf die nächste Stunde. Genaue Aufgabenstellung s. Hausaufgabe auf dem Stundenblatt.

Worksheet No. 1 siehe Stundenblatt

Approximate order of composition of Shakespeare's works

Period	Comedies	Histories	Tragedies	Poetry
1584	Comedy of Errors Taming of the Shrew Two Gentlemen of Verona	1, 2, 3 Henry VI Richard III King John	Titus Andronicus*	Venus and Adonis Rape of Lucrece *"epic poems"*
I 1592				
1594	Love's Labour's Lost			
II	Midsummer-Night's Dream Merchant of Venice Merry Wives of Windsor Much Ado About Nothing As You Like it	Richard II 1 Henry IV 2 Henry IV	Romeo and Juliet	Sonnets
1599		Henry V		
III	Twelfth Night Troilus and Cressida Measure for Measure All's Well That Ends Well		Julius Caesar* Hamlet Othello Timon of Athens Lear Macbeth Antony and Cleopatra* Coriolanus*	
1608				
IV 1613	Pericles Cymbeline Winter's Tale *"romances"* Tempest	Henry VIII		

*The Roman Plays

Aus: Peter Alexander (ed.). *The Tudor Edition of William Shakespeare. The Complete Works*

14

History of Rome (6th century B.C. – 14 A.D.)

1. **Tyranny**
   6th century B.C.

   Brutal tyranny under king Tarquin the Proud

2. **Republic**
   509

   Revolution, led by Lucius Junius Brutus, ancestor of
   Marcus Brutus

   509 – 60

   Government formed of two consuls (elected by the people) and
   a Senate. Two tribunes as 'ombudsmen' for the common
   people. Evenual decline of the republic.

3. **Caesar's rule**
   60

   First triumvirate: Pompey, Crassius, Caesar

   48

   Caesar defeats Pompey (at Pharsalia) and later his two sons

   48 – 44

   Caesar reigns with almost absolute power, loved by the people

   44, March 15

   Caesar's assassination by Brutus, Cassius and others

4. **Interregnum**
   43

   Second triumvirate: Octavius, Antony, Lepidus

   42

   Defeat of Caesar's murderers at Philippi

   31

   Octavius defeats Antony at Actium and conquers Alexandria

5. **Octavius' rule**
   27 B.C. – 14 A.D.

   Octavius adopts the titles of 'Princeps' (= the chief one),
   'Caesar' (cf. 'Kaiser') and 'Augustus' (= the majestic)

THE ROMAN EMPIRE-44BC

territory in
Roman possession

ATLANTIC
OCEAN

ROME

PHILIPPI

BLACK SEA

•SARDIS

NORTH AFRICA

MEDITERRANEAN SEA

Aus: *Oxford School Shakespeare.* Julius Caesar

2. Stunde:
Elisabethanisches Englisch

Didaktische Vorbemerkungen

Die kursorische Beschäftigung mit elisabethanischem Englisch in dieser Stunde hat vor allem zwei Funktionen: Zum einen soll sie den Schülern etwas die Scheu vor der vermeintlich unverständlichen, da „altenglischen", Sprache nehmen, zum anderen sollen ihnen elementare Kenntnisse über einige wichtige Merkmale des elisabethanischen Englisch vermittelt werden, um ihnen den späteren Umgang mit dem Originaltext zu erleichtern. Die Stunde basiert wesentlich auf der Hausaufgabe.

Im Sinne einer allmählichen Einführung beginnt die Stunde mit der Betrachtung eines inhaltlich und auch sprachlich einfachen elisabethanischen Sachtextes (vgl. Worksheet No. 1). Weitere Merkmale des elisabethanischen Englisch werden dann anhand von Beispielen (vgl. Worksheet No. 2) aus Shakespeare-Dramen (vorwiegend aus JC) erarbeitet. Am Ende der Stunde wird kurz auf die unterschiedliche Verwendung von Blankvers und Prosa bei Shakespeare eingegangen.

Da die Ergebnisse der Sprachuntersuchungen sehr umfangreich sind, teilt der Lehrer sie am Ende der Stunde zusammengefaßt als Handout aus. Trotzdem werden während des Unterrichts Teilergebnisse an die Tafel geschrieben, damit die Aufmerksamkeit der Schüler gewährleistet ist und ihr Gedächtnis nicht überstrapaziert wird.

Die allgemeine Charakterisierung des elisabethanischen Englisch (vgl. Zusatztext S. 18) kann als Informationsgrundlage für einen kurzen, die Stunde einführenden Lehrervortrag (oder ein Schülerreferat) verwendet werden.

Verlauf der Stunde

1. Unterrichtsschritt:
Sprache eines elisabethanischen Sachtextes

Zu Beginn der Stunde wird die *gemeinsame* Hausaufgabe (vgl. Worksheet No. 1) besprochen. Die von den Schülern gefundenden sprachlichen Auffälligkeiten werden zunächst an einer Seitentafel gesammelt oder auf einer Folie unterstrichen. Anschließend werden gemeinsam sprachliche Kategorien und Subkategorien (vgl. linke Spalte des Handout) zu den ermittelten Abweichungen vom modernen Englisch gesucht und an der Tafel festgehalten. Im Handout sind die Beispiele aus dem Sachtext mit * markiert.

2. Unterrichtsschritt:
Sprachproben aus Shakespeares Dramen

Im folgenden wird die *arbeitsteilige* Hausaufgabe (vgl. Worksheet No. 2) sukzessive besprochen (Gruppen A–C). Die Schüler unterstreichen in der linken Spalte des Worksheet die gefundenen sprachlichen Auffälligkeiten und schreiben jeweils den entsprechenden Kommentar in die rechte (noch leere) Commentary-Spalte. Anschließend werden die Ergebnisse wieder kategorisiert und die Kategorien an der Tafel festgehalten.

16

3. Unterrichtsschritt:
Bildersprache

Die Schüler sollen in diesem Schritt anhand von zwei kurzen Auszügen aus zentralen Passagen von JC erste Bekanntschaft mit Shakespeares Bildersprache machen. Die Gruppe D trägt die Ergebnisse ihrer Hausaufgabe vor, die Bezeichnungen der drei Bildtypen (personalization, metaphor, comparison) werden als Kategorien an der Tafel festgehalten.

4. Unterrichtsschritt:
Funktion von Vers und Prosa

Die Schüler sollen zunächst anhand der Beispiele No. 2 und No. 4 im Worksheet No. 2 erkennen, daß Shakespeare im gleichen Drama Vers und Prosa verwendet. Mit Hilfe einer kurzen metrischen Analyse wird das allgemeine Versschema des Blankverses („blank verse" = reiner, d. h. reimloser Vers; fünfhebiger Jambus: xx́xx́xx́xx́xx́[x]) erarbeitet und vom Lehrer kurz auf die unterschiedliche Verwendung von Vers und Prosa in Shakespeares Dramen eingegangen. Zum Abschluß der Stunde wird das Handout ausgeteilt und vom Lehrer, falls nötig, erläutert.

Worksheet No. 1

The True Reportory of the Wracke

For fource and twenty houres the storme in a restlesse tumult, had blowne so exceedingly, as we could not apprehend in our imaginations any possibility of greater violence, yet did wee still finde it, not onely more terrible, but more constant, fury added to fury, and one storme urging a second more outragious
5 then the former [...]. Sometimes [...] shrieks in our Ship amongst women, and passengers, not used to such hurly and discomforts, made us looke one upon the other with troubled hearts, and panting bosomes: our clamours dround in the windes, and the windes in thunder. Prayers might well be in the heart and lips, but drowned in the outcries of the Officers: nothing heard that
10 could give comfort, nothing seene that might incourage hope... the Sea swelled above the Clouds, and gave battell unto Heaven. It could not be said to raine, the waters like whole Rivers did flood in the ayre.

(William Strachey, 1609)

Aus: Suerbaum: a.a.O.

Annotations
apprehend fear – *hurly* tumult – *ayre* air.

Die Elisabethaner und die Sprache

In der Regierungszeit Elisabeths ist nicht nur, bedingt durch den neuerrungenen Platz unter den führenden Nationen, durch relativen Wohlstand und durch kräftige Propaganda der Behörden, ein Anwachsen des nationalen Selbstbewußtseins zu verzeichnen, es vollzieht sich gleichzeitig ein Wandel in
5 der Einstellung zur Sprache und eine Zunahme der kunstsprachlichen Aktivitäten.
Schon in der Blütezeit des englischen Humanismus zu Anfang des 16. Jahrhunderts war das Augenmerk in verstärktem Maße auf die Sprache gelenkt worden, allerdings vorwiegend auf die klassischen Sprachen, insbesondere
10 das Lateinische. Obwohl einige Humanisten ihre Schriften in der Muttersprache publizierten, hatte das Englische, die Vulgärsprache, im ganzen noch wenig gegolten. Es war vor allem Mittel der alltäglichen Verständigung, dessen man sich ohne besonderes Bewußtsein eines Potentials an Gestaltungsmöglichkeiten bediente. Ausdruck dieser Haltung waren unter anderem die
15 Humanistenschulen, deren Lehrplan ganz auf das Latein fixiert war und Englisch als Fach nicht kannte.
Im Laufe des Jahrhunderts begann man dann immer mehr, die Möglichkeiten zu entdecken, die in der eigenen Sprache steckten. Das Englische wurde zum bevorzugten Medium der gehobenen Sprache. In allen Gattungen der Poesie
20 wurde am Ausbau des Mediums gearbeitet. Sogar ein Teil der Gelehrten gab jetzt der Muttersprache den Vorzug. "I honor the Latin, but I worship the English", sagte der Humanist Richard Mulcaster.
Der Prozeß des Zuwachses, von den Elisabethanern *augmentation* genannt, spiegelt sich in der Entwicklung des Vokabulars. Gegen Ende des 16. Jahr-
25 hunderts ist der schriftlich belegte Wortschatz des Englischen mehr als doppelt so hoch als zu Anfang. Dabei wird die Sprache, die durch die Überschneidungen des romanischen und des germanischen Anteils ohnehin vokabelreich ist, vor allem durch Begriffe vermehrt, die dem Lateinischen – auch den nachantiken Fachsprachen – entnommen sind. Andere Zugänge
30 entstehen durch Neubildung, Funktionserweiterung (z. B. Gebrauch von Substantiven in verbaler Funktion), Kombination oder durch Aufnahme von Dialektwörtern in die Schreibsprache.

Nur ein Teil des neuen Vokabulars gehört der Gemeinsprache an. Der Großteil gehört – jedenfalls zunächst – der Sondersprache eines bestimmten
35 Autors an, der zu einmaliger oder wiederholter Verwendung seine eigenen Begriffe prägt. Bei Begriffen, die generell im Umlauf sind, ist oft die Auslegung der Bedeutung individuell. Das elisabethanische Englisch ist also in stärkerem Maße als das moderne Englisch ein Konglomerat von Eigensprachen mit relativ schwach ausgeprägter gemeinsamer Grundlage. [...]
40 Shakespeares Sprache ist, auch mit den Maßstäben ihrer eigenen Zeit gemessen, ein Sonderfall; sie ist nicht die notwendige oder naheliegende Konsequenz aus einer bestimmten historischen Situation. Aber dieser Sonderfall wird durch die damalige Position der Sprache als eines gesellschaftlichen Phänomens ermöglicht und gefördert. Shakespeares Sprache gehört in eine
45 Zeit, in der sich sprachliche Experimente und Sondersprachen leicht durchsetzten, weil man bereit war, jedem, der etwas Neues mit der Sprache anstellte, Gehör zu schenken. Sie ist ferner das Werk eines Autors, der damit rechnen konnte, daß sein Publikum sprachlichen Produktionen einen hohen Unterhaltungs- und Vergnügungswert zusprechen würde, daß es einem Wort-
50 gefecht mit geradezu sportlichem Interesse folgte und einen Monolog nicht nur als Sinngebilde, sondern auch als virtuose Spracharie goutierte.
Die Sprache ist schließlich auf ein Publikum zugeschnitten, das auch noch dem Exzeß gegenüber tolerant blieb und sich bereitwillig überfordern ließ. Wir tendieren heute dazu, das elisabethanische Publikum zu überschätzen und ihm
55 ein volles Verständnis der Shakespeareschen Sprache zuzutrauen. In Wirklichkeit übersteigen viele Dialogpartien die Grenzen des bei einmaligem Hören zu Entschlüsselnden. Kein elisabethanischer Theaterbesucher hat alle wesentlichen Aussagen des *Hamlet* erfaßt. Man war jedoch zur Anstrengung und zur Bescheidung mit partiellem Verständnis bereit.
60 Weil diese Vorbedingungen erfüllt waren, konnte Shakespeare die Freiheit, die der objektive Sprachzustand durch die Offenheit der Syntax und Semantik und durch das riesige Potential an Wörtern bot, voll ausnutzen.

Aus: Suerbaum, Ulrich: *Shakespeares Dramen.* Düsseldorf: August Bagel Verlag 1980, S. 83–85.

Characteristics of Elizabethan English

[Für die Schülerkopien rechte Seite abdecken.]

<u>Example</u>

[Group A]
No. 1   (JC I.1)

Flavius
Hence! home, you idle creatures, get you home.
Is this a holiday? What! know you not,
Being mechanical, you ought not walk
Upon a labouring day without the sign
5 Of your profession? Speak, what trade art thou?
First Citizen
Why, sir, a carpenter.
Marullus
Where is thy leather apron and thy rule?
What dost thou with thy best apparel on?
You, sir, what trade are you?
Second Citizen
10 Truly, sir, in respect of a fine workman, I am but,
as you would say, a cobbler.
Marullus
But what trade art thou? Answer me directly.
Second Citizen
A trade, sir, that I hope I may use with a safe con-
science, which is indeed, sir, a mender of bad soles.
Marullus
15 What trade, thou knave? Thou naughty knave,
what trade?

<u>Commentary</u>

2   Frage ohne „to do", vgl. 19

5   „thou" in negativem Kontext, vgl. 15
     „art" statt „are", vgl. dagegen 9

7   „thy" statt „your", vgl. 8
8   „dost" statt „do"
9   „are" und „you", vgl. dagegen 5

13–15   pun „soul" – „sole" [soul]

20

Second Citizen
Nay, I beseech you, sir, be not out with me; yet, if you be out, sir, I can mend you.
Marullus
What mean'st thou by that? Mend me, thou saucy fellow!
20 And do you now put on your best attire?
And do you now cull out a holiday?

17 „nay" statt „no", „to beseech"

19 Frage ohne „to do", vgl. 2

21 Fragen mit „to do"

[Group B]
No. 2   (JC I.2)

Portia
I must go in. [Aside] Ay me, how weak a thing
The heart of woman is! O Brutus,
The heavens speed thee in thine enterprise!
25 Sure the boy heard me. – Brutus hath a suit
That Caesar will not grant. – O, I grow faint. –
Run, Lucius, and commend me to my lord;
Say I am merry. Come to me again,
30 And bring me word what he doth say to thee.

25 „thee" in positivem Kontext;
    „thine" statt „your"

26 „hath" statt „have"

30 „doth" statt „does"

No. 3   (JC I.2)

Caesar
Would he were fatter! But I fear him not.
Yet if my name were liable to fear,
I do not know the man I should avoid
So soon as that spare Cassius. He reads much,

31 Verneinung ohne „to do"

33 Verneinung mit „to do"

21

No. 4 (JC I.2)

Casca
35 Marry, before he fell down, when he perceiv'd the common herd was glad he refus'd the crown, he pluckt me ope his doublet, and offer'd them his throat to cut. An I had been a man of any occupation, if I would not have taken him at a word, I would I might
40 go to hell among the rogues. And so he fell.

[Group C]
No. 5 *Cassius*
Caesar said to me 'Dar'st thou, Cassius, now Leap in with me into angry flood, And swim to yonder point?'

No. 6 (As You Like It, II.4)
I cannot go no further.

No. 7 (The Tempest I.2)
45 I will rend an oak and peg thee in his knotty entrails.

No. 8 (JC IV.3)
Cassius
When Caesar liv'd, he durst not thus have mov'd me.
Brutus
Peace, peace! You durst not so have temped
50 him.

35 „marry" = „fürwahr"

38 „An" = „if"

41 „dar'st" = „darest" = „dare" Elision

44 Doppelte Verneinung zur Emphase

46 „his" statt „its"

47 „durst" = Präteritum zu „dare"

[Group D]
No. 9 (JC II. 1, 77–85)

Brutus

O conspiracy,
Sham'st thou to show thy dang'rous brow by night,
When evils are most free? O, then by day
Where wilt thou find a cavern dark enough
55 To mask thy monstrous visage? Seek, none,
conspiracy;
Hide it in smiles and affability!
For if thou path, thy native semblance on,
Not Erebus itself were dim enough
60 To hide thee from prevention.

personalization:
„conspiracy" = a person

No. 10 (JC IV.3, 110–113)

Brutus

O Cassius, you are yoked with a lamb,
That carries anger as the flint bears fire;
Who, much enforced, shows a hasty spark,
And straight is cold again.

61 metaphor: Brutus = lamb
62 comparison:
anger is like a flint that . . .

Annotations

being mechanical (3) being a workman – *rule* (7) measure – *apparel* (8) clothes – *cobbler* (11) incompetent workman – *attire* (21) dress – *cull out* (22) select – *speed* (25) give success to – *suit* (26) request – *spare* (34) thin – *marry* (35) ‚fürwahr' – *pluckt me ope his doublet* (37) opened his garment – *man of any occupation* (38) man of action – *rend* (45) tear out – *peg* (46) drive into – *durst* (47) past of 'dare' – *shame* (52) to be ashamed – *evil* (53) evil spirit – *affability* (57) pleasantness – *path* (58) walk around – *semblance* (58) appearance – *Erebus* (59) dark region under the earth – *prevention* (60) discovering – *yoked* (61) united – *flint* (62) ‚Feuerstein'.

I. Some Characteristics of Elizabethan English

1. Orthography

Additional '-e-'	* "storme", "bosomes", "onely"
Deviating spelling	* "battell", "ayre" [= air]
Different spellings of the same word	* "dround" – "drowned"
Capitals for emphasis	* "Rivers", "Ships"
Additional commas	
Elision	"Sham'st" statt "shamest"

2. Grammar

2.1 Pronouns

Personal pronoun (2nd pers. sing.)	Besides "you" (nominative/accusative also "thou" (nom.) and "thee" (acc.) Difference in usage: "you" is the neutral form, "thou/thee" in positive or negative emotional context
Possessive pronoun	"thy/thine" instead of "your" "his" instead of "its"

2.2. Modal auxiliaries (2nd pers.)

"can"/"could"	"thou canst"/"couldst"
"shall"/"should"	"shalt"/"shouldst" (cf. in the Bible: "Thou shalt not kill")
"will"/"would"	"wilt"/"wouldst"
"may"/"might"	"mayst"/"mightst"
"dare"/"dared"	"darest"/"durst"

2.3 Verbs (2nd/3nd pers. sing. pres.)

	Instead of or besides the modern forms you will find:
Full verbs	"-eth": "he loveth"
"to be"	"you art" (pres.), "you wert/warst" (past)
"to do"	"you dost", "he doth"
"to have"	"you hast", "he hath"

3. Syntax

	Besides the modern forms you may find:
question/negative sentence	no use of "to do": – "know you not?" – "I fear him not"

double negative (for greater emphasis)	"I cannot go no further"
double comparative	"more greater"
inversion, following "yet"	* "yet did we … find"
past with "to do"	* "the waters … did flood"
ellipsis	* "nothing [was] heard that …"
	* "nothing [was to be] seen that …"

4. Semantics

Now archaic or extinct words	* "hurly" for "tumult"
	* "so … as" for "so … that"
	* "reportory" for "report"
	"to beseech" (lit.) = to ask earnestly or urgently
	"prithee" (arch.) = please
	"forsooth/in faith" = in truth
	"aye/nay" = yes/no
	"and/an": sometimes = 'if'
	"marry" = "fürwahr"
	"hence" = "hinweg"

5. Style/Imagery

5.1. Style in general	Rich in images, ornate, artificial, emotionally charged, e.g.: "shrieks made us looke one upon the other with troubled hearts, and panting bosoms"
	* "the Sea swelled above the Clouds, and gave battell unto Heaven"
5.2. Imagery metaphor comparison	"O Cassius, you are yoked with a lamb. That carries anger as the flint bears fire"
personalization	"O conspiracy, sham'st thou to show thy dang'rous brow by nigth …?"
pun (witty play upon words e.g.: Two different meanings of a homophone)	[soul] = "soul" and "sole" ('Schuhsohle'). Cf. JC I.1.13–17

*: Beispiele aus Worksheet No. 1

II. Shakespeares usage of verse and prose

Blank verse: five-stress iambic line without a rhyme xx́xx́xx́xx́xx́(x)
Verse: serious themes, people of high standing
Prose: comical themes, low people, reports

3./4. Stunde:
Das elisabethanische Theater

Didaktische Vorbemerkungen

Diese Doppelstunde soll den Schülern eine kurze Einführung in das elisabethanische Theater und sein gesellschaftliches Umfeld (Reputation, Zuschauer) geben. Generell sollte dabei bedacht werden, daß „trotz generationslanger Forschungsarbeit [...] immer noch nicht in allen wesentlichen Punkten geklärt [ist], wie es in einem elisabethanischen Theater aussah und wie die Aufführungen bühnentechnisch durchgeführt wurden" (Suerbaum: a.a.O, S. 67).

Didaktisches Strukturprinzip dieser Stunde ist die Gegenüberstellung von elisabethanischem und heutigem Theater. Im Mittelpunkt stehen die spezifischen Merkmale der elisabethanischen „apron stage" (im Gegensatz zur modernen Guckkastenbühne) und die sich daraus ergebenden dramaturgischen Konsequenzen.

Zunächst werden anhand von zeitgenössischen Texten das schillernde gesellschaftliche Image des Theaters und die heterogene Zusammensetzung seines Publikums erarbeitet. Der zweite Teil der Doppelstunde konzentriert sich dann auf die Form des elisabethanischen Theaters und dessen dramaturgische Möglichkeiten und Grenzen.

Die wichtigsten Ergebnisse der einzelnen Unterrichtsschritte werden in Form eines tabellenartigen wachsenden Tafelanschriebs (vgl. Tafelanschrieb im Stundenblatt) festgehalten.

Das Programm für diese Doppelstunde ist sehr umfangreich. Gegebenenfalls kann der 2. Unterrichtsschritt entfallen.

Verlauf der Doppelstunde

1. Unterrichtsschritt:
Das Image des elisabethanischen Theaters

Sachinformation: Die gesellschaftliche Position des elisabethanischen Theaters unterscheidet sich erheblich von der heutiger Theater:

„Im elisabethanischen London ist die Position des Theaterwesens anders als in modernen Städten. Das Theater hat noch keinen anerkannten Platz als Kultur- und Bildungsinstitut oder überhaupt als Träger wichtiger gesellschaftlicher Funktionen. Es ist kommerzielles Unterhaltungstheater, rein privatwirtschaftlich betrieben, von den Behörden drangsaliert oder geduldet, aber auf keinen Fall Ausdruck kommunalen Selbstgefühls oder Gegenstand bürgerlichen Stolzes." (Suerbaum: a.a.O, S. 54)

Die fragwürdige Rolle der Theater kommt auch deutlich in ihrer geographischen Randlage (vgl. Stadtplan auf Worksheet No. 1) zum Ausdruck. Shakespeares berühmtes Globe Theatre in Southwark befand sich in einem ausgesprochenen Vergnügungsviertel, zu dem neben Theatern auch Attraktionen wie Dirnen und Bärenhatz (vgl. Hentzner-Text, Worksheet No. 2) gehörten. Trotzdem – oder gerade deswegen (?!) – hatten die Theater großen Zulauf und waren in aller Munde. Das Platzangebot allein der sechs „public theatres" zu Shakespeares Zeiten (jeweils 1500–3000 Zuschauer) war prozentual zur damaligen Londoner Bevölkerung (200 000–250 000 Einwohner) deutlich höher als heute. Hinzu kamen noch einige „private theatres" in früheren Klöstern (vgl. das „Blackfriars") oder in Adelshäusern, in denen bei künstlicher Beleuchtung vor einem weniger zahlreichen Publikum („Blackfriars" ca. 700 Zuschauer) gespielt wurde.

Worksheet No. 1 siehe Stundenblatt

A German Traveller Reports

Without the city are some theatres, where English actors represent almost every day comedies and tragedies to very numerous audiences; these are concluded with a variety of dances, accompanied by excellent music and the excessive applause of those that are present.

5 There is still another place, built in the form of a theatre, which serves for the baiting of bears and bulls. They are fastend behind, and then worried by those great English dogs and mastiffs, but not without great risk to the dogs from the teeth of the one and the horns of the other; and it sometimes happens they are killed upon the spot. Fresh ones are immediately supplied in the places of

10 those that are wounded or tired. [...]

At these spectacles and everywhere else, the English are constantly smoking the Nicotian weed which in American is called *Tobaca* [and] fruits, such as apples, pears and nuts, according to the season, are carried about to be sold, as well as wine and ale.

From *Travels in England* by Paul Hentzner (1598)
Aus: *Life-Language-Literature.* Stuttgart: Ernst Klett Verlag 1982, S. 222

Annotations
without here: outside – *to bait* make an animal angry intentionally – *to worry* here: to make angry – *mastiff* a type of large powerful dog (Bulldogge)

Methodische Hinweise: Die „Map of London" (vgl. Worksheet No. 1) erlaubt eine anschauliche Einführung in den Themenbereich. Im fragend-entwickelnden Verfahren können aus dem Stadtplan einige wesentliche Fakten (Randlage, Nähe zu anderen ungeliebten Einrichtungen wie Gefängisse und Krankenhäuser, Teil des Amüsierbetriebs) erarbeitet werden.

Die Ergebnisse werden dann durch die gemeinsame Lektüre des Textes „A German Traveller Reports" (vgl. Worksheet No. 2) bestätigt und vertieft.

2. Unterrichtsschritt:
Argumente der Theatergegner

Sachinformation: Die geographische Lage der Theater ist ein Indiz für die zweideutige Reputation, die die Theater in offiziösen kirchlichen und staatlichen Kreisen genossen. Während die z.T. schon puritanisch orientierte Kirche vor allem durch die Theater moralische Verderbnis befürchtete, sahen die Politiker und die tonangebende Mittelschicht in den Theatern und den dort gespielten Stücken in erster Linie eine Gefahr für Ruhe und Ordnung.

A Letter to the Archbishop

[Our most humble duties to Your Grace remembered. Whereas by the daily and disorderly exercise of a number of players and playing houses erected within this City, the youth thereof is greatly corrupted and their manners infected with many evil and ungodly qualities by reason of the wanton and
5 profane devises represented on the stages by the said players, the apprentices and servants withdrawn from their works, and all sorts in general from the daily resort unto sermons and other Christian exercises to the great hindrance of the trades and traders of this City and profanation of the good and godly religion established amongst us.] To which places also do usually resort great
10 numbers of light and lewd-disposed persons as harlots, cutpurses, cozeners, pilferers, and such like and there under the colour of resort to those places to hear the plays devise divers evil and ungodly matches, confederacies and conspiracies, which by means of the opportunity of the place cannot be prevented nor discovered, as otherwise they might be. In consideration
15 whereof we most humbly beseech Your Grace [...] to vouchsafe us your good favor and help for the reforming and banishing of so great evil out of this City, which ourselves of long time though to small purpose have so earnestly desired and endeavored by all means that possibly we could.

Sir William Roe
Lord Mayor of the City of London
25 February 1592

Aus: *Life-Language-Literature.* Stuttgart: Ernst Klett Verlag 1982, S. 223

Annotations
whereas common formula used in introductions to laws, petitions, etc. – *wanton* wild, uncontrolled, improper – *devise = device* plan; here: story, action of a play – *to withdraw* to take away – *resort* here: visit – *lewd* immoral, obscene – *harlot* (old use) a prostitute – *cutpurse* (old use) pickpocket – *cozener* a person that cheats and deceives by trickery – *pilferer* thief – *under the colour of resort* here: pretending to visit – *match* forming of pairs – *confederacy* group of people joined for a certain purpose – *conspiracy* a plan made by a group to do something unlawful – *to beseech* to ask urgently – *to vouchsafe* to be kind enough to give – *to banish* to prohibit under penalty – *to endeavour* to try

Das Theater war daher für Autoren und Akteure eine nicht ganz ungefährliche Angelegenheit: Thomas Nashe und Ben Jonson kamen wegen der politischen Satire „The Isle of Dogs" (1597) zusammen mit den Schauspielern ins Gefängnis.

Angesichts dieser massiven Opposition war es nicht verwunderlich, daß den Theatern nur eine kurze Blütezeit beschert war. 1642 wurden von den Puritanern (Oliver Cromwell) sämtliche Theater geschlossen, und selbst nach der Restauration von 1660 wurden von Charles II lediglich zwei Theater in London lizensiert.

Was für die Institution des Theaters galt, galt in modifizierter Form für die gesamte Literatur der damaligen Zeit, die im 16. Jahrhundert noch um ihre Anerkennung als wesentlicher Bestandteil der öffentlichen Kultur zu kämpfen hatte. Innerhalb der Literatur wiederum nahm das Drama den untersten Rangplatz ein: Zu seiner Zeit wurde Shakespeare weniger wegen seiner Dramen als wegen seiner Versdichtungen geschätzt.

Methodische Hinweise: In diesem Schritt sollen anhand eines zeitgenössischen Textes die wichtigsten Argumente der Theatergegner erarbeitet werden. Da der Text „A Letter to the Archbishop" (vgl. Worksheet No. 3) für die Schüler sprachlich nicht einfach ist, sollte der Text zunächst zu Hause erarbeitet werden. Im Unterricht wird dann der Inhalt des Textes anhand einer Leitfrage (vgl. Stundenblatt) zunächst in Stillarbeit und dann im Unterrichtsgespräch erschlossen. Als Arbeitsgrundlage dient neben dem Worksheet eine Folie mit den ersten 8 Zeilen [Kernsatz] des Textes.

Die wichtigsten Ergebnisse ergänzen den bisherigen Tafelanschrieb.

3. Unterrichtsschritt:
Das Publikum des elisabethanischen Theaters

Das wesentlichste Charakteristikum des Publikums, seine große Heterogenität, wird gemeinsam anhand des Textes „The Globe Audience" (vgl. Worksheet No. 4) erarbeitet. Abschließend wird kurz diskutiert, wie ein damaliger Autor einem so stark gemischten Publikum am besten gerecht werden konnte.

Auch hier werden die wichtigsten Ergebnisse an der Tafel festgehalten.

4. Unterrichtsschritt:
Vergleich: elisabethanisches und heutiges Theater

Bevor sich der Unterricht den dramaturgischen Besonderheiten der elisabethanischen Bühne zuwendet, werden zunächst, in einer Art Zwischenbilanz, die bisher erarbeiteten Merkmale des elisabethanischen Theaters mit den Gegebenheiten des modernen verglichen. Bei diesem Vergleich ist allerdings zu berücksichtigen, daß man im modernen Theater natürlich die Verhältnisse der elisabethanischen Bühne weitgehend imitieren kann. Der Unterschied zwischen beiden Theaterformen wird am deutlichsten, wenn man sich eine realistische Inszenierung vor Augen hält. Der Unterrichtsverlauf orientiert sich dabei an den im Tafelanschrieb vorgegebenen Kategorien; die Ergebnisse werden in der zweiten Spalte des Tafelanschriebs eingetragen.

The Globe Audience

The Globe audiences probably represented a wider range of citizens than have attended theatres in Britain since that time. The cost of admission was low, to attract as large a number as possible. The 'groundlings', who stood on the ground in the orchestra where there were no seats, were made up for the most
5 part of shopkeepers, craftsmen and members of what might be called the lower bourgeoisie. There were also the apprentices, rowdy young men given to exhibitionism and liable to create disturbances out of sheer exuberance of spirit, but genuine lovers of the theatre, and usually well educated. There were also gentlemen of various degrees, professional men, courtiers, and
10 members of the nobility. They would occupy twopenny or threepenny seats in the gallery. The members of the nobility would present themselves conspicuously in seats at the side of the stage itself or in shilling 'rooms'. Women were among the audience, often the respectable wives of tradesmen, a fact which surprised foreign visitors to London. The capacity of the Globe was
15 probably about two thousand or a little more, and a typical audience would consist of at least one thousand people.

From *Literary Landscapes of the British Isles* by David Daiches and John Flower, Paddington Press, New York and London 1979
Aus: *Life-Language-Literature*. Stuttgart: Ernst Klett Verlag 1982, S. 224.

Annotations

orchestra here: the main floor of a theatre – *craftsman* skilled workman, such as carpenter, goldsmith – *exhibitionism* the behaviour of a person who wants to be looked at and admired – *exuberance* state of being very lively and cheerful – *courtier* noble at the court of a king – *twopenny, threepenny, shilling* old currency – *conspicuous* noticeable, attracting attention

5. Unterrichtsschritt:
Die elisabethanische „apron stage"

Die Besonderheiten der elisabethanischen Bühne werden in einem kurzen Schülerreferat thesenartig vorgetragen. Basis sind die Texte auf Worksheet No. 5 und 6. Der Referent sollte seine Ausführungen, soweit möglich, an der Skizze des Swan Theatre (vgl. Worksheet No. 6)

konkretisieren und die wesentlichsten Stichworte seines Referats entweder während seines Vortrags oder vorher an die Tafel schreiben, so daß am Ende seines Vortrags auch ein Tafelanschrieb vorliegt, der ggf. vom Lehrer im Unterrichtsgespräch korrigiert wird. Die dramaturgischen Konsequenzen der „apron stage" werden im folgenden Unterrichtsschritt vertieft und ergänzt.

Worksheet No. 5 (Grundlage für das Schülerreferat)

The Atmosphere in an Elizabethan Theatre

What would strike a modern eye most about Shakespeare's theatre was its smallness. The auditorium of the Globe was probably about 55 feet square, that is approximately the size of a lawn tennis court; and this included the stage, which jutted right out among the audience, and was some 43 feet wide
5 by about 27 feet long. The play was therefore performed almost in the middle of the theatre, the groundlings standing on three sides of the stage, which was raised three or four feet off the floor, while the seats for those who could afford them were ranged in three tiers of galleries round the walls, and in some theatres stools could even be hired for accommodation on the stage
10 itself. The whole atmosphere must have been extraordinarily intimate and domestic, especially when we remember that the personnel both of the company and of the audience was far more permanent than anything conceivable in modern London. Each member of the cast would be as familiar to the spectators as the individuals of a local football team are to-day to a crowd on
15 the home ground. Under such conditions acting and drama were very different from anything we know now. And to understand Shakespare, [...] we must think ourselves back into that little room at the Globe or its predecessors, in which his dramas were first given by a team of players, moving and speaking on a bare platform surrounded by a ring of faces only a few yards
20 away.

Aus: Wilson, J. D.: *The Essential Shakespeare.* Cambridge University Press 1946.

Worksheet No. 6 (Grundlage für das Schülerreferat)

Shakespeare's Theatre

Drama, of all forms of art, is most immediately affected by material circumstance. The poet or the novelist can wait for recognition, perhaps for years, but a dramatist, and especially one who is also a sharer in the playhouse and company which produces his plays, cannot afford a failure. He must please his
5 public or he will go bankrupt. He appeals, not to future ages, but to the audience of the afternoon. His plays therefore must be written to suit the stage on which they will be performed, the company which is to act them, and the audience which will pay to see them.
Until James Burbage built the Theatre in 1576, Elizabethan players had no
10 permanent home. They were accustomed to act on a variety of stages. They gave private performances in the great halls of noblemen's houses or in one of the Queen's palaces, or the Inns of Court, and they acted in public in Town Halls and inn yards, or in any place where they could erect a stage and collect a crowd.

15 The stage used by travelling players
was simple – a platform of boards
resting on trestles or barrels,
with a curtained booth at
the back where the actors
20 could change their costumes
or wait for the cue for entrance.
[...]
Within the outer walls there
were three tiers of galleries,
25 looking down on the stage
and the yard where the
poorer spectators stood.
The stage itself, technically
known as an 'apron stage',
30 jutted out into the yard, so
that when the house was
full the players were surrounded on three sides.
Over the stage the 'shadow'
35 or roof protected the players from the rain.

The structure of the stage considerably affected the form of Elizabethan plays.
In the modern theatre the actor is separated from his audience by a curtain
which conceals or reveals the whole stage. Moreover, he acts in bright light
40 before spectators hidden in a darkened auditorium. On the apron stage the
actor came forward in daylight into the midst of his audience. He and they
were thus, as it were, fused into a common experience. The device of
soliloquy was not, as on the modern stage, embarrassingly artificial, but a
45 quite natural communication as a character explains his thoughts and intentions to those immediately before him. As there was no need for him to shout,
the greatest subtlety of voice, gesture, and expression was possible. Nor
needed he to speak slowly; in that small auditorium every word could easily be
heard, and the spectators were eager and trained listeners.
50 Apparently there was no scenery apart from an occasional property gate, tree,
or the like, and plays were acted in daylight. The Elizabethan actor was thus
without the lighthing, scenery, sound effects, and other realistic or symbolic
adjuncts of the modern stage. In their place he gained his effects by a direct
assault on the emotions and the imagination of the spectators. Poetry was thus
55 a natural medium for dramatic speech, especially at exalted moments, and a
good actor could carry his audience with him by the emotional force of
rhetoric.

The action was continuous. A scene ended when all the actors had gone off
the stage and a new set of characters came on. There was thus a quick
60 continuity of performance with no break in the illusion. As there was no
scenery, so there was no limit to the number of scenes. Usually the exact
locality of the scene was unimportant. When it was necessary Shakespeare
showed it in the dialogue.
'What country, friends, is this?' Viola asks.
65 'This is Illyria, lady,' the sea captain answers.
But for the most part a simple property or garment was sufficient. Chairs or
stools showed indoor scenes; a man wearing riding-boots was a messenger; a
king wearing his armour was on the field of battle; a watchman carrying a
lantern indicated the streets of a city at night. The most important difference
70 between the modern and the Elizabethan theatre is that on the public stages
there was no curtain to divide the stage from the auditorium. [...]
On the other hand costumes were sometimes lavish and imposing. When in
1601 the Admiral's Men produced a play of Cardinal Wolsey they bought 'two
pile velvet of carnadine at twenty shillings a yard, satins at twelve shillings and
75 taffetas at twelve and six'. The bill for material alone came to £21 in money of
the day. An inventory of costumes in the *Henslowe Papers,* probably of the
same date as the inventory of properties, lists eighty-four garments of various
kinds, most of them magnificent, such as 'a short velvet cloak embroidered
with gold and gold spangles', 'a crimson robe striped with gold, faced with
80 ermine', 'a cardinal's gown'.
There seems to have been little attempt at historical accuracy; the Romans in
Julius Caesar and *Coriolanus* wore doublets, cloaks, and large hats; Cleopatra
was tight-laced in a 'busk'. In *Troilus and Cressida,* Hector and Ajax fought
by the rules of medieval combat and in *Lear* (nominally a prehistoric play)
85 Edgar wore a closed helmet which covered his face.

Aus: Harrison, G. B.: *Introducing Shakespeare.* Harmondsworth [3]1966, pp. 120, 139–141, 144.

6. Unterrichtsschritt:
Dramaturgische Gegebenheiten von
„apron stage" und „Guckkastenbühne"
(„fourth-wall stage")

Die materiellen Unterschiede zwischen
beiden Bühnenarten sind offensichtlich. In
diesem abschließenden Schritt kommt es
daher darauf an, die spezifischen dramaturgischen Möglichkeiten und Grenzen
der elisabethanischen gegenüber der heutigen Bühne herauszuarbeiten. Der Lehrer sollte deshalb in einem relativ eng
geführten Unterrichtsgespräch die Schüler
dazu auffordern, sich möglichst konkret
vorzustellen, was es z. B. für eine Auffüh-
rung bedeutet, wenn man keinen Vor-
hang oder kaum Kulissen hat oder wenn
die Zuschauer sehr viel näher an der Bühne sind als in großen modernen Theatern.
Das Gerüst für dieses Gespräch ergibt sich
aus den Hauptpunkten des Schülerrefe-
rats. Die Ergebnisse werden im Tafelanschrieb festgehalten.

5. Stunde:
Der Handlungsverlauf des Dramas

Didaktische Vorbemerkungen

Ziel dieser ersten Stunde nach der häuslichen Lektüre des Dramas ist die Erarbeitung einer groben Handlungsübersicht. Da die folgende Analyse des Dramas im wesentlichen chronologisch vorgeht, ist es wichtig, daß die Schüler immer auch den gesamten Handlungsablauf vor Augen haben. Dies soll dadurch ermöglicht werden, daß auf der Basis der häuslichen Lektüre des Dramas eine Übersicht über seine Handlung in Form einer Graphik erarbeitet und diskutiert wird.

Notes on interpretation

The question "What is JC about?" is not so trivial as it appears at first sight. It is a rather unique and for many critics puzzling feature of this drama that the 'title hero' already dies in the middle of the play. Attempts at 'normalizing' the drama by referring to Caesar's post-mortal existence as a ghost are not very convincing, as Caesar's ghost is not very prominent in the last two acts. It is true that Caesar's party is the winning team in the end, but it is a very tricky question whether cold manipulators of power like Antony or Octavius can be accepted as Caesar's legitimate spiritual heirs or successors. It is more likely that the drama was titled as it is because Caesar was better known in Elizabethan times than Brutus. There is certainly more about Brutus than about Caesar in this drama.

On the story level the drama deals with the fate of a conspiracy against Caesar. We are witnesses of its coming-into-being (act I), its consolidation (act II), its crisis (act III) and its gradual decline (act IV) and final defeat (act V). In this respect the drama follows rather exactly Gustav Freytag's formula, although there is little retardation in the fourth act, where everything seems already lost for the conspirators. The drama's tragic irony lies in the fact that the conspirators lose in the end although they have reached their main goal, Caesar's murder. Therefore, the real turning point is not the murder but the effect of Antony's forum speech. Cynics and modern election managers may feel confirmed in their opinion that in politics words count more than deeds.

Of course, there is more to it. The conspiracy mainly fails in the end because Brutus, with his strong moral scruples and his ensuing fatal decisions, is the wrong man for this job. So we may conclude that JC is about the tragic defeat of a high-minded idealist. But by only slightly changing the accent (words again!) we may come to the opposite conclusion that impractical idealists like Brutus only create chaos and civil war – as is shown in the drama – and should therefore be adequately punished – as they are in the drama. This ambiguity is inherent in JC and can be either accepted as such by the reader/spectator or dissolved by his personal decision in favour of one of the two parties.

Verlauf der Stunde

1. Unterrichtsschritt:
Erarbeitung einer Handlungsübersicht

Ziel dieses und des folgenden Schritts ist die Erarbeitung des Tafelanschriebs. Zunächst werden, unter Rückgriff auf die Hausaufgabe, Überschriften zu den einzelnen Akten gesucht. Ziel dabei ist es, daß die Schüler die einzelnen Akte als spezifische Teile der Gesamthandlung

„Geschichte einer Verschwörung" erkennen und entsprechende Überschriften finden. Wahrscheinlich werden sich verschiedene Vorschläge für Überschriften auf das Schicksal einzelner Figuren oder spezifische Szenen beziehen. Solche Antworten sind, für sich genommen, durchaus sinnvoll, aus ihnen ergibt sich aber keine einheitliche Gesamthandlung.

2. Unterrichtsschritt:
Detaillierung der Handlungsübersicht

Der in den Aktüberschriften skizzierte grobe Handlungsrahmen wird nun konkretisiert in Form von zwei „Schicksalskurven" oder Handlungslinien für die beiden feindlichen Parteien. Eine positive Steigung der Kurve steht für eine Verbesserung der Situation, eine negative Steigung für eine Verschlechterung der Situation einer Partei. Bei der Erstellung der Kurven werden gleichzeitig die wichtigsten Ereignisse auf ihnen markiert (vgl. Tafelanschrieb). Wir beginnen mit der im Vordergrund des Dramas stehenden Partei der Verschwörer.

3. Unterrichtsschritt:
Analyse des Handlungsverlaufs

Dieser Schritt schließt unmittelbar an den zweiten an – er kann sich auch mit ihm teilweise überschneiden, wenn im Verlauf des zweiten Schritts von den Schülern entsprechende Fragestellungen angesprochen werden. Die Analyse des Handlungsverlaufs anhand des Tafelanschriebs sollte sich auf folgende Punkte konzentrieren:
– Welches sind warum die wichtigsten Ereignisse?
– Formale Analyse des Handlungsverlaufs: Zwei antagonistische, thematisch und personell aufeinander bezogene Handlungsstränge, die zunächst beide als steigende Handlungen beschrieben werden können, sich dann aber nach dem Wendepunkt des Dramas gegenläufig entwickeln.
– Bewertung des Dramenendes: Hat das Drama einen positiven oder einen negativen Ausgang? Hier sollte deutlich werden, daß die Antwort auf diese Frage vom Rezipienten abhängt. In diesem Zusammenhang kann auch kurz die Frage andiskutiert werden, ob der Dramentitel wirklich die Hauptfigur bezeichnet.

Hausaufgabe

Intensive Vorbereitung von I.2.38–178. Diese Passage ist Textbasis der folgenden Stunde und spielt auch noch in der nächsten Stunde eine wichtige Rolle. Der Szenenausschnitt sollte von den Schülern sprachlich und inhaltlich vor allem unter der Fragestellung betrachtet werden, mit welchen Mitteln Cassius versucht, Brutus zur Teilnahme an der Verschwörung zu überreden? Diese rhetorische Thematik wird später, bei der Analyse der Forumsszene, wiederaufgenommen.
Bei der Erläuterung der Hausaufgabe sollte den Schülern klargemacht werden, daß von nun an ausschließlich der englische Text Grundlage der Hausaufgaben ist.

6. Stunde:
Techniken der Überredung I

Didaktische Vorbemerkungen

Im Mittelpunkt dieser Stunde und z.T. auch der folgenden Stunde steht der zu Hause vorbereitete Dialog zwischen Cassius und Brutus (I.2.33–178), in dem Cassius versucht, Brutus zur Teilnahme an der Verschwörung zu gewinnen. Dieser Textausschnitt ist in dreifacher Hinsicht für das Drama von großer Bedeutung:
– Zum einen handelt es sich um eine für die Handlung zentrale Szene.
– Darüber hinaus ist Cassius' Gesprächsführung eine rhetorische Meisterleistung.
– Schließlich dient diese Szene der Einführung zweier Hauptfiguren.

In dieser Stunde wird der Textausschnitt unter rhetorischen bzw. Aspekten des persuasiven Sprachgebrauchs analysiert. Dieser Einstieg in die konkrete Textarbeit wurde gewählt, weil eine solche Analyse eine besonders intensive Auseinandersetzung mit dem Text erfordert. Die Analyse rhetorischer Mittel wird später bei der Betrachtung der Forumsreden von Brutus und Antonius wieder aufgenommen.
Nach einer kurzen Rekapitulation des Stellenwertes der Szene in der Dramenhandlung wird die Passage abschnittsweise besprochen. Der erste Abschnitt des Dialogs (33–90) dient Cassius vor allem auch dazu herauszufinden, wie Brutus zu Cäsar und dessen politisch dominierender Position steht. In den folgenden beiden Abschnitten (91–132 und 136–162) steht dann der persuasive Aspekt im Vordergrund. Gefragt wird jeweils, mit welchen – unterschiedlichen – Mitteln Cassius versucht, Brutus in die gewünschte Richtung zu lenken, und wie er seine Strategie nach den jeweiligen Reaktionen des Dialogpartners ausrichtet. Dabei sollten die einzelnen Abschnitte jeweils in Stillarbeit kurz vergegenwärtigt werden. Die Ergebnisse werden als „techniques of persuasion" an der Tafel festgehalten.

Notes on interpretation

Conspiracy is under any circumstances a delicate topic of conversation. This is all the more true if you are not sure about your partner's views on it. Cassius, therefore, has to be very careful at the beginning of this dialogue not to give himself away before he knows for certain that Brutus at least shares his intense misgivings about Caesar's dominant political position. Only if this test provides a positive result can Cassius really come to the point.
Brutus, Caesar's friend, has also reason to be reserved: Although he is worried about Caesar's seeming aspirations to kingship, he has not yet made up his mind about his course of action.
Cassius starts with an appeal to their friendship and a reproach for Brutus' recent neglect of it. Brutus' answer is more open and explicit than is afforded by the communicative situation: He admits that he is "vexed by passions" (40/41) and "with himself at war" (47) – both clear indications of a severe inner struggle – but insists on the privacy of the subject matter of his troubles ("conceptions only proper to myself", 42). Cassius in turn accepts this excuse (which, by the way, confirms their friendship) and signalizes readiness to commune his hitherto "buried worthy cogitations" under these conditions.
But before coming to the point, Cassius makes a second attempt to bring Brutus out of his shell by referring to other important people who are worried about

Brutus' apparent indifference (or more flattering: his "hidden worthiness"). At the same time, he approaches the real subject of this conversation by referring to "this age's yoke" (62). This expression still leaves open the cause and nature of this "yoke". It is only very indirectly linked with – "immortal" (!?) – Caesar.

Brutus' answer shows that he knows pretty well what Cassius is driving at ("danger", 64), but he pretends (thus reproaching Cassius) that nothing of the kind could be found in himself ("that which is not in me", 66). Cassius does not accept Brutus' denial and offers his services ("I, your glass", 69) as a psychoanalyst to disclose Brutus' yet unconscious ideas. At the same time he stresses his seriousness and reliability.

Then pure chance comes to Cassius' aid and eagerly he takes up Brutus' critical comment on people's shouting and tries to pin down Brutus on it (82/83). Brutus' reaction reveals that the subject matter of his inner struggle is his ambivalent attitude to Caesar. He shows that the balance of his judgement is turning against his friendship with Caesar in favour of honour, which for him is closely linked with the "general good" (86).

Now Cassius feels safe enough to come to his real point, his deep worries about Caesar's predominant political position, which is for him a question of damaged honour and self-esteem. Nothing could show the essential difference between these two men more clearly than their different conceptions of "honour": For Brutus, it means political responsibility for the general good, i. e. for others, for Cassius, honour is a question of individual status. Therefore, his long argument against Caesar which follows lacks all political perspective and is solely motivated by an intense feeling of envy and ensuing hatred of Caesar, his superior. Cassius'

motivation is summarized best by Caesar's following judgement on Cassius: "Such men as he be never at heart's ease whiles they behold a greater than themselves, and therefore are they very dangerous." (209–211)

The structure of Cassius' argument against Caesar is rather obvious: He questions Caesar's superior position mainly from two points of view:

From the angle of personal merit, Caesar's predominance is in Cassius' opinion unjustified because Caesar is in no way better than e. g. Brutus or Cassius (98–100, 143–151). On the contrary – that is the main rhetorical point of Cassius' two extensive examples of Caesar's weakness (the swimming contest 105–116 and Caesar's fever 120–130) –, he is physically even their inferior. Both examples culminate effectively in rhetorical amazement about the grotesque disparity between the weak 'real' man and his high public position:

– And this man ("tired Caesar") is now become a god; and – the much stronger – Cassius is a wretched creature, and must bend his body . . ." (116–119).
– "Ye gods! it doth amaze me a man of such a feeble temper should so get the start of the majestic world." (129–131).

Seen from the angle of Roman history, Caesar's single predominance means a fatal break with a long and glorious tradition. At the same time it is a serious symptom of the decadence of Roman nobility (151–158). This seemingly collective accusation is then, by Cassius reference to Brutus' famous ancestor, turned against his friend.

The central aim of Cassius' extensive argument is a strong appeal to Brutus to do something at last against Caesar's undeserved predominance: "Men at some time are masters of their fate: The fault, dear

Brutus, is not in our stars, but in ourselves, that we are (resp.: that we behave like) underlings." (140–143)

In contrast to Cassius' passionate arguing, Brutus' reactions have more the character of an official statement than of a spontaneous answer in a private conversation. The real message of these rather stilted and sibyllic words seems to be the following: We must talk about this important matter again, I will think about it, and you may be sure that I will live up to my noble reputation if things develop further – which I think is rather likely – in that fatal direction ("these hard conditions", 175). Cassius' curt and slightly sarcastic final statement reflects his irritation at his friend's rather noncommittal answer.

Verlauf der Stunde

1. Unterrichtsschritt:
Bedeutung der Textstelle

Zu Anfang dieser Stunde sollte zunächst kurz geklärt werden, welche dramentechnische Funktion (Einführung zweier Hauptfiguren) und welche Bedeutung für die Gesamthandlung (wichtiger Schritt bei der Vorbereitung der Verschwörung) die im Mittelpunkt der Stunde stehende Textstelle (I.2.33–178) hat.

2. Unterrichtsschritt:
Analyse von I.2.33–90

Die Analyse der ersten, vorbereitenden Phase dieses Überredungsdialogs konzentriert sich auf zwei Fragen:
- Wie findet Cassius Brutus' Einstellung zu Cäsars wachsender Macht heraus?
- Mit welchen Mitteln versucht Cassius, Brutus in die gewünschte Richtung zu lenken.

Die Ergebnisse werden an der Tafel festgehalten. Die Dynamik des Dialogs, das wechselseitige Reagieren auf die jeweiligen Reaktionen des Partners, wird deutlicher, wenn jeweils auch Alternativen zu den ‚tatsächlichen' Reaktionen mit bedacht werden. Wenn Brutus z. B. die ihm von Cassius vorgeworfene Vernachlässigung seiner Freunde mit gesundheitlichen Problemen erklärt hätte, hätte Cassius sein Ziel aufgeben müssen.

3. Unterrichtsschritt:
Analyse von I.2.91–162

Die Analyse dieser Passage wird in zwei Teilschritten (91–132 und 136–162) vorgenommen. Untersucht werden soll jeweils, mit welchen Mitteln Cassius versucht, Brutus von der Notwendigkeit einer Aktion gegen Cäsar zu überzeugen. Trotz dieser Aufteilung in zwei Teilschritte sollte die globale Struktur von Cassius' Argumentation gegen Cäsar nicht außer acht gelassen werden. Die Ergebnisse werden an der Tafel festgehalten.

4. Unterrichtsschritt:
Analyse von I.2.163–178

Zum Abschluß der Analyse wird diskutiert, inwieweit Cassius sein Ziel erreicht hat. Dabei sollte auch auf II.1, wo Brutus seine Entscheidung vor sich selbst begründet, verwiesen werden.

Hausaufgabe

Im Mittelpunkt der folgenden Doppelstunde steht Cäsar, die Titelfigur. In arbeitsteiliger Hausarbeit sollen die entsprechenden Szenen bzw. Szenenausschnitte von den Schülern daraufhin untersucht werden, mit welchen Mitteln welche Aspekte von Cäsar jeweils dargestellt werden.

Gruppeneinteilung:
1. Gruppe: I.1.31–33, 70–77; I.2.1–25; II.2.1–56.
2. Gruppe: I.2.80–163 (schon bekannt); II.1.10–27; II.2.57–128.
3. Gruppe: I.2.236–275; I.3.72–89; III.1.32–77.

7./8. Stunde: „Charakter" Cäsars

Didaktische Vorbemerkungen

In den folgenden drei Stunden stehen die Charaktere (und deren Darstellung) der drei Hauptfiguren Cäsar, Brutus und Cassius im Vordergrund. Unter „Charakter" einer Figur wird dabei nicht eine statische Menge fester Eigenschaften verstanden, sondern ein dynamisches Vorstellungsgebilde, das sich in der Anschauung des Lesers/Zuschauers bildet und ständig verändert. Es bezieht sich nicht nur auf Eigenschaften, sondern auch auf Einstellungen, Ziele und Motive der Figuren und deren Beziehungen zu anderen Figuren. Wesentliches Ziel dieser Figurenbetrachtungen ist es daher nicht, „den" Charakter einer Figur zu „erkennen", sondern das im Laufe des Dramas entfaltete Spektrum von Interpretationsmöglichkeiten der Figuren zu erarbeiten. Aus dieser Zielsetzung ergeben sich zwei Prinzipien für das weitere Vorgehen:
1. Da die Hauptfiguren immer neue Facetten zeigen, müssen sie (mit Ausnahme Cäsars) durch das ganze Drama hindurch verfolgt werden.
2. Es ist jeweils auch zu prüfen, wie zuverlässig ein bestimmtes Charakterisierungsmittel an einer bestimmten Stelle ist. Konkret bedeutet dies, daß nicht nur zwischen verschiedenen Mitteln (vor allem: Selbstaussage, Urteile anderer, Verhalten/Handeln) zu unterscheiden ist, sondern daß auch deren Stellenwert und Funktion im jeweiligen konkreten Szenenkontext zu beachten sind.

Im Mittelpunkt der vorliegenden Doppelstunde steht Cäsar. Bevor die konkrete Textanalyse beginnt, werden als theoretisches Grundgerüst kurz die wichtigsten dramatischen Charakterisierungsmittel erarbeitet bzw. wiederholt. In den folgenden Unterrichtsschritten werden dann die einzelnen zu Hause arbeitsteilig vorbereiteten Textpassagen im Hinblick auf die Frage untersucht, welche Charaktereigenschaften jeweils auf welche Weise zur Darstellung gelangen. Die einzelnen Ergebnisse werden an der Tafel festgehalten.

Notes on interpretation

The picture of Caesar presented to us is ambivalent if not flatly contradictory: On one occasion (Lupercal ceremonies) he seems to believe in religious rites, on another he totally ignores the warnings of a soothsayer. To Calphurnia he behaves rather rudely in public; the conspirators, though, are kindly welcomed on the morning of the fatal ides of March. Antony deplores him as "the noblest man that ever lived in the tide of times" (III.1.257/258), Cassius on the other hand portrays Caesar as "tired Caesar" (I.2.116), refers to "his coward lips" (I.2.123), and compares him with a "sick girl" (I.2.129).
What are we to make of this strange puzzle, the parts of which do not seem to fit together properly? Was Shakespeare unable to portray a character coherently or do we start from the false expectation that characters in a drama are to be coherent?

Let us try to solve this puzzling riddle by a closer examination of the pertinent passages.

Already in the very first scene we are confronted with opposing opinions on Caesar: The citizens' reckless joy about Caesar's triumph (32/33) is confronted with Flavius' deep worries about Caesar's triumphant career. The two points of view, though, are not really contradictory when we consider the persons who give the judgements and to what aspects of Caesar's personality they refer. The citizens are just glad about the extra holiday provided, as it were, by Caesar and about Caesar's victory which they interpret as their own victory. (Compare the respective reactions of football fans to a victory of "their" team.) The tribunes' point of view is more political and also encompasses possible future developments. They intone the conspirators' central criticism of Caesar, which is less directed against Caesar's present behaviour than against his possible development: "who else would soar above the view of men, and keep us all in servile fearfulness" (75–77). Flavius' prognosis combines two important key conceptions in a causal way, i. e. Caesar's present superhuman position ("above the view of men") and his expected future tyrannic behaviour. This hypothesis, which to Cassius is already a fact (Caesar = "a god", "like a Colossus", Cassius = a "wretched creature", a "petty man" who must bend his body), is also central to Brutus' self-justification in II.1, which we will discuss later.

The assumption that Caesar is ambitious and rather unscrupulous seems to be supported by Casca's report on Caesar's threefold renunciation of the crown ("but to my thinking, he was very loath to lay his fingers off it" [the crown], I.2.242/243) and the secret execution of the two tribunes, I.2.287/288.

Caesar's behaviour in public is in many ways apt to create antipathy on part of the reader/spectator. His permanent bossiness during his first appearance on the stage (I.2) and the corresponding servility of his train may be partly explained as consequences of his position. But his boastfulness and conceit in public ("I am constant as the northern star", III.1.60; "Know, Caesar doth not wrong", III.1.47) and in private ("Danger knows full well that Caesar is more dangerous than he", II.2.44–47) verge on megalomania and are as difficult to pardon as his rude exposure of Calphurnia in public during the feast of Lupercal (I.2).

Caesar, as a private man, disrobed of his public image, is less impressive: He has severe physical defects (one deaf ear, epilepsy) and is not stronger than other ordinary men (that is Cassius' main point in I.2). In addition, he is at times rather indecisive (cf. the scene with Calphurnia, where he changes his mind twice), he is susceptible to flattery (cf. his change of mind after Decius' re-interpretation of Calphurnia's dreams in II.2.283–290; cf. also II.1.209–211), and he is uncertain in his judgement about dreams, prodigies, and ceremonies (cf. Cassius in II.1.193–200; also Caesar's contradictory attitude to superstition in I.2 and II.2). With respect to this last aspect, it is a form of tragic irony that Caesar does not follow the different warnings as regards his vanity (tickled by Decius) and his megalomania.

These rather negative aspects of Caesar's personality are more or less compensated for by Brutus' and especially Antony's high esteem of him ("the noblest man that ever lived", III.1.257) and Caesar's capacity for deep friendship, which is tragically disappointed in the end: "Et tu, Brute? – Then fall, Caesar!".

Summarizing, we may say that the portrait of Caesar is generally characterized by two ambivalences, namely a mixture of good and bad qualities and a disparity between his private and his public appearance. For Brutus, at least, both ambivalences are identical: He accepts and loves Caesar as a private man but fears him as a public man or politician strong enough to plan and execute his murder.

Verlauf der Stunde

1. Unterrichtsschritt:
Charakterisierungsmittel

Zu Anfang der Doppelstunde sollen folgende hauptsächlichen dramatischen Mittel zur Figurendarstellung erarbeitet bzw. (wenn schon aus dem Deutschunterricht bekannt) vergegenwärtigt werden:
– Selbstaussage oder Selbstcharakterisierung
– Handlungen von Figuren, die für den Leser/Zuschauer Rückschlüsse auf den Charakter der Figuren zulassen. Dazu gehören: das verbale Verhalten (was eine Figur sagt und ggf. wie sie es sagt, also sprachlicher Inhalt und sprachliche Form) und das aktionale Verhalten einer Figur (was sie tut).
– Aussagen anderer Figuren über eine Figur.

Bei allen drei Kategorien sollte auch deutlich werden, daß man die Textbefunde oft nicht „at their face value" nehmen darf, sondern interpretieren muß, z. B.: Ist eine Selbstaussage oder eine Fremdaussage zutreffend bzw. aufrichtig oder nicht? Was läßt sich mit welcher Sicherheit aus einer bestimmten Handlungsweise einer Figur schließen?
Schließlich sollte auch klar werden, daß sich die einzelnen Fälle nicht notwendig wie Puzzlesteine zu einem einheitlichen

Bild fügen, sondern daß sie sich durchaus auch widersprechen bzw. gegenseitig in Frage stellen können.

2. Unterrichtsschritt:
Einführung Cäsars

Wie oft bei Shakespeare (vgl. etwa „Hamlet" oder „Macbeth") tritt die Titelfigur in der ersten Szene nicht selbst auf, sondern wird indirekt eingeführt. Die beiden Textpassagen (I.1.31–33, 70–77) werden zunächst still gelesen und dann im fragend-entwickelnden Verfahren besprochen. Wichtig ist, daß bereits hier die ambivalente Darstellung von Cäsars Charakter deutlich herausgestellt wird.

3. Unterrichtsschritt:
Cäsars erster Auftritt

Obwohl die Szene (I.2.1–25) kurz ist, ist sie relativ komplex, da es verschiedene Ebenen zu beachten gilt, die zusammen gesehen wiederum kein einheitliches Bild von Cäsar ergeben. Die Szene wird zunächst von der Kassette vorgespielt und dann anhand des schriftlichen Textes besprochen.

4. Unterrichtsschritt:
Die Perspektive der Verschwörer

In diesen drei Szenen (I.2.80–163, 236–275; I.3.72–89; II.1.10–27) wird Cäsar wieder aus einer neuen Perspektive, der der Verschwörer, gezeigt. Der erste der drei Szenenausschnitte ist schon aus der vorhergehenden Stunde bekannt, er wird hier allerdings unter einer anderen Fragestellung betrachtet. Die Passagen sollten in bezug auf das durch sie vermittelte Cäsarbild kritisch analysiert werden, da Verschwörer naturgemäß nichts Positives über ihr zukünftiges Opfer zu sagen haben (Brutus ist da eine seltene Ausnahme!).

Die Ergebnisse der arbeitsteiligen Hausarbeit werden von den einzelnen Gruppen vorgetragen und anschließend diskutiert.

5. Unterrichtsschritt:
Cäsar privat

In dieser Szene (II.2) wird als letzte neue Perspektive Cäsar im privaten Bereich gezeigt. Bei der Analyse dieser Szene sollte der Unterschied zu Cäsar als „public figure" deutlich herausgearbeitet werden.
Die relativ umfangreiche Textpassage wird in drei Teilschritten (1–56, 57–107, 108–128) behandelt. Beim zweiten Teil sollte auch kurz auf Decius' erfolgreiche Überredungskunst eingegangen werden. Der dritte Teilschritt kann sehr kurz gefaßt werden.

6. Unterrichtsschritt:
Cäsars „imperial style"

Im Mittelpunkt steht hier (III.1.32–77) die Analyse von Cäsars Sprachstil als Ausdruck seines grotesk übersteigerten Selbstbewußtseins. Der Szenenausschnitt wird zunächst von der Kassette vorgespielt und dann fragend-entwickelnd behandelt. Zur Ergänzung wird noch kurz die Textstelle III.1.255–258 betrachtet, in der Antonius von Cäsar als „the noblest man that ever lived in the tide of times" spricht.

7. Unterrichtsschritt:
Zusammenfassung

Zum Abschluß der Stunde wird anhand des Tafelanschriebs eine zusammenfassende Charakterisierung von Cäsar vorgenommen. Dabei sollten die beiden nicht ganz deckungsgleichen Ambivalenzen (privat vs. öffentlich, gute vs. schlechte Eigenschaften), die das hervorstechende Merkmal der Titelfigur sind, deutlich herausgestellt werden.

Hausaufgabe

Die erste vorläufige Charakterisierung von Cassius und Brutus in der folgenden Stunde basiert im wesentlichen auf zuvor schon unter anderen Fragestellungen behandelten Textstellen (I.2.29–178, I.2.191–215, I.2.309–323, I.3.53–130, I.3.157–160, II.1.35–58), die von den Schülern zu Hause arbeitsteilig (eine Gruppe für Brutus, eine für Cassius) im Hinblick auf deren Aussagewert für den Charakter der jeweiligen Figur untersucht werden. Darüber hinaus sollen alle den Dialog zwischen Brutus und seiner Frau Portia (II.1.234–303) unter der genannten Fragestellung und vor dem Hintergrund des schon bekannten Dialogs Cäsar-Calphurnia (II.2.8–56) untersuchen.

9. Stunde:
Die Figuren Brutus und Cassius

Didaktische Vorbemerkungen

In dieser Stunde stehen Cäsars beide Hauptgegner, Brutus und Cassius, zum ersten Mal im Mittelpunkt der Betrachtung. Das dabei erarbeitete Bild der beiden Figuren wird in den folgenden Stunden – dies gilt vor allem für Brutus – ergänzt und modifiziert: Während in der folgenden Stunde Brutus mit seinen Entscheidungsproblemen allein im Vordergrund steht, bietet die 11. Stunde (Besiegelung der Verschwörung) die Gelegenheit, die Gegensätzlichkeit der beiden Verschwörer weiter herauszuarbeiten. Zum dritten Mal thematisiert wird dann der Kontrast beider Figuren bei der Behandlung der „quarrell scene" (IV.3).
Die Stunde beginnt mit auf die Hausaufgabe bezogener Gruppenarbeit, anschließend werden die Ergebnisse der beiden

Gruppen vorgetragen und diskutiert. Da beide Gruppen im wesentlichen die gleichen Bezugstexte haben, können sie auch ihre Ergebnisse wechselseitig beurteilen. Im dritten Unterrichtsschritt wird gemeinsam der Dialog zwischen Brutus und Portia (II.1.234–303) analysiert. Die Ergebnisse werden jeweils an der Tafel festgehalten und am Ende zusammengefaßt.

Notes on interpretation

Usually, we judge people either by their aims, motives or by the means they use to reach their aims: We attribute a bad character to someone whose aims and motives we consider immoral, selfish or foolish, presupposing at the same time that he will use questionable means anyway. All of us know, on the other hand, the age-old discussion of whether (good) ends justify (questionable) means. These two categories – means and ends – may help us to describe the main differences between Cassius and Brutus.

As far as methods are concerned we have had the occasion in our first review of I.2.29–178 to admire Cassius' rhetorical gifts. In his conversation with Casca (I.3.53–130), Cassius gives another splendid performance of this talent to move people in the desired direction by sheer rhetoric. Here, Cassius makes practical use of Cicero's epistemological scepticism ("But men may construe things after their fashion", I.3.34) by talking Casca into the belief that the thunderstorm is neither the result of a "civil strife in heaven" (I.3.11) nor of men's 'sauciness with the gods' (I.3.12) but ("the true cause") a severe godly warning "unto some monstrous state" (I.3.71), meaning the consequences of Caesar's growing power.

But Cassius does not rely solely on his verbal powers, but also on manipulative tricks as his "letter action" (cf. its planning in I.2.310–323 and its success in II.1.35–58) shows. At the same time, Cassius is conscious of the moral doubtfulness of his manipulation of his friend Brutus: In Brutus' place, he would not have liked to be treated in this way (cf. I.2.315/316) and his in this context slightly cynical advice ("that noble minds keep ever with their likes", I.2.311/312) implies that he considers himself not a "noble" mind as he does Brutus.

In order to manipulate people successfully the absence of scruples is not sufficient – you also need a good insight into other people's characters, especially into their weaknesses. Even without Caesar's pertinent remark on Cassius ("He is a great observer, and he looks quite through the deeds of men", I.2.203/204) his dealings with Brutus and Casca give ample proof that Cassius has all the requirements necessary for the successful manipulation of others.

Apart from Cassius' methods, his aims, too, are not beyond all moral doubts. Although he frequently refers to Rome's now endangered glorious republican past (cf. I.2.151–162 and "our fathers' minds are dead", I.3.82) and the impending dangers of tyranny (in which case he would not hesitate to commit suicide, cf. I.3.89–99), we never totally lose the suspicion that Cassius' actions are less governed by ideals and values like "honour", "freedom", or "the general good" (cf. in contrast Brutus' frame of mind), but by intense hate and personal envy (cf. I.2.94–150). It is Caesar again who most clearly pins down Cassius' moral insufficiency: "Such men as he be never at heart's ease whiles they behold a greater than themselves, and therefore are they very dangerous." (I.2.209–211)

Brutus, in contrast, appears as a frank, honest, unselfish and scrupulous idealist, motivated only by positive values like "honour" or "the general good". His nobleness of mind is not only testified by Cassius but is reflected by the high reputation he enjoys with the people, a quality which makes his participation in the conspiracy absolutely mandatory: "O, he sits in all the people's hearts; and that which would appear offence in us his countenance, like richest alchemy, will change to virtue and to worthiness." (I.3.157–160) Casca's remark, by the way, also points to the manipulative use one can make of such well-reputed persons as token men, whose presence may glorify even evil deeds in the general opinion.

In contrast to Elizabethan times, Brutus' dedication to "honour" will be less appealing to modern spectators/readers than his loving and equal partnership with his wife Portia which reflects, in contrast to Caesar's domination relationship to Calphurnia, a deep and essential humanity.

In spite of all his nobility Brutus is not quite free from vanity. It is shrewd Cassius who detects this weakness and successfully exploits it for his own purposes. He does this with his "letter action" ("I will this night [...] writings, all tending to the great opinion that Rome holds of his name", I.2.316–320): "Three parts of him is ours already" (I.3.154/155) he boasts to Casca and his prognosis does prove right (cf. II.1.45–58)!

Nobility of mind, Cassius' analysis of Brutus also seems to imply, often goes hand in hand with a certain naivety which easily falls victim to manipulations by less noble minds, such as Cassius.

In the passages so far analyzed, the two leading conspirators are depicted as morally contrasting characters: Brutus appears as an honest, noble, scrupulous and slightly naive idealist; Cassius, in contrast, as an unscrupulous, selfish, and very competent schemer. A careful analysis of the further course of the drama will show whether and to what extent this preliminary characterization does justice to these two characters.

Verlauf der Stunde

1. Unterrichtsschritt:
Vergleich der Hausaufgaben

Zu Beginn der Stunde diskutieren die Mitglieder beider Gruppen die Ergebnisse ihrer Hausarbeit und einigen sich auf einen Sprecher, der das in der Gruppe erarbeitete Ergebnis vorträgt.

2. Unterrichtsschritt:
Charakterisierung von Cassius und Brutus

Zunächst werden die Ergebnisse der „Cassius-Gruppe" im Plenum vorgetragen, diskutiert und an der Tafel festgehalten. In der gleichen Reihenfolge wird dann bei Brutus vorgegangen.

3. Unterrichtsschritt:
Brutus und Portia (II.1.234–303)

Der von allen zu Hause vorbereitete Dialog wird zunächst von Kassette vorgespielt und dann im Hinblick auf Brutus' Charakter besprochen. Als Kontrastfolie dient dabei der zuvor schon besprochene Dialog zwischen Cäsar und Calphurnia (II.2.8–56). Der Vergleich beider Szenen sollte sich nicht ausschließlich auf die beiden Hauptfiguren beziehen, sondern zunächst auf den Vergleich zweier – für die männlichen Partner allerdings jeweils charakteristischer – Partnerschaftsbeziehungen.

4. Unterrichtsschritt:
Brutus vs. Cassius

Abschließend wird anhand des bisherigen Tafelanschriebs eine kurze kontrastive vorläufige Charakterisierung der beiden Figuren erarbeitet.

Hausaufgabe

In der folgenden Stunde werden Brutus' vier Entscheidungsmonologe (II.1.1–85) besprochen. Da die Monologe zwar kurz, aber sprachlich und gedanklich z. T. sehr schwierig sind, wird als Hausaufgabe „nur" eine gründliche sprachliche Vorbereitung der Textstelle erwartet.

10. Stunde: Brutus' Entscheidung

Didaktische Vorbemerkungen

Monologe haben im klassischen Drama vor allem die Funktion, das Innenleben, insbesondere innere Probleme und Konflikte, einer Figur offenzulegen, und treten oft an entscheidenden Stellen eines Dramas (vgl. „Hamlet") auf. Im Mittelpunkt dieser Stunde steht Brutus' Entscheidung zur Teilnahme an der Verschwörung, die in vier kurzen aufeinanderfolgenden Monologen (II.1.10–85) dramatisch realisiert ist.
Obwohl die endgültige Entscheidung erst im zweiten Monolog (II.2.44–58) fällt, liegt der dramatische Akzent auf dem ersten Monolog (II.1.10–34), in dem sich Brutus mit möglichen Begründungen und Rechtfertigungen für eine Verschwörung gegen Cäsar auseinandersetzt. Die argumentative Analyse dieses Monologs steht daher im Mittelpunkt des ersten Teils der Stunde.

Im zweiten Teil der Stunde werden die restlichen drei Monologe betrachtet. Bei der Analyse aller vier Monologe sollte jeweils auch gefragt werden, was sie über Brutus' Charakter aussagen. Die Stunde schließt mit der Erstellung eines zusammenfassenden Tafelanschriebs.

Notes on interpretation

Brutus' decision on his participation in the conspiracy (and consequently, in Caesar's murder) is dramatized in four subsequent monologues (II.1.10–85). This fact alone is a clear indication of how difficult this decision is for Brutus, and this mainly for two reasons:
– Caesar is Brutus' friend and
– Brutus abhors all forms of violence.
Therefore, to participate in the conspiracy means for Brutus to be ready to kill a personal friend by detestable means (cf. the later dichotomy 'sacrificers vs. butchers', II.1.166).

We would expect that only absolute certainty about the necessity of the murder for the general good could induce Brutus to make such a crucial decision. Consequently, Brutus begins his monologue with the very resolute statement "It must be by his death" (II.1.10). But what seems to be at first the expression of deadly certainty soon turns out to be a nagging question ("Is Caesar's death necessary?") which is not really convincingly answered in the end (neither for Brutus himself nor for the reader/spectator).
Brutus' main problem is that he can find no fault (cf. "to speak truth of Caesar", 19) with Caesar's past and present behaviour, neither in the private (11) nor in the public sphere (119/20). Thus, he can base his decision only on a hypothesis about Caesar's future behaviour after being

crowned. The highly speculative quality of his inner reasonings corresponds with the frequent use of the conditional ("may/might") and the doubtful reliance on proverbs ("It is the bright day that brings forth the adder", 14) and "common proof" (21). This last argument ("lowliness is young ambition's ladder", 22) is, by the way, somewhat unfair, for it interprets the apparent absence of a quality (i. e. ambition) as especially hard evidence for its existence. It is the kind of argumentative trap which some people ascribe to psychoanalysts: "So you feel that you are in good psychic health? Well that is exactly your trouble, that you do not realize that you are in urgent need of therapy."

Taking into account the shakiness of Brutus' "evidence" for Caesar's future negative development, the conclusion "So Caesar may not" is as convincing as Brutus' "So Caesar may" (27). Therefore, Brutus is quite right in thinking that the case needs some "fashioning" before being succesfully communicable to the public or being convincing enough to himself. This monologue is really a tragic example of someone talking himself into believing something he is not really convinced of, its last few lines being a recipe for how to deceive oneself.

Quite obviously, Brutus is not yet at all certain of the justification for the intended course of action. Therefore, Brutus is only ready to make his final decision after the reception of Cassius' mock letters which, ironically, betray their author in their very wording (compare "see thyself", 46 with I.2.68). These letters are not only flattering for Brutus but give him the subjective conviction that other people see the same danger as he does. Thus, Brutus' decision is overshadowed by an aura of (self-)deception and manipulation: The letters are fakes and are very

subjectively interpreted by Brutus ("Thus must I piece it out", 51; cf. the motive of "fashioning" in 30). And again, Brutus looks to the future when he decides on the – as such honourable – condition that "the redress will follow" (57). The trouble is that he must act before he knows whether his condition will be fulfilled.

Apparently, Brutus lacks firm conviction and the capacity for clear moral reasoning. His participation in the conspiracy seems to be more the result of Cassius' manipulation (cf. also: "Since Cassius first did whet me against Caesar", 61) than of his own volition.

While the first two monologues deal mainly with Brutus' rational problems, the last two monologues give, in a series of impressive images, an insight into his agitated emotional situation which reflects his rational uncertainty. Only in the last four lines does Brutus find his way to practical considerations ("Hide it in smiles and affability", 82). His readiness to accept disguise may be understood as an indication that he has now identified with the conspiracy.

Altogether, the four monologues convey the distinct impression that Brutus is neither mentally nor emotionally sufficiently prepared for what he is going to do, i. e. to murder a friend for inconclusive reasons.

Verlauf der Stunde

1. Unterrichtsschritt:
Brutus' Selbstrechtfertigung (II.1.10–34)

Brutus' Hauptproblem besteht darin, daß er sich nicht sicher ist, ob Cäsar wirklich so gefährlich ist, daß man seine Ermordung moralisch rechtfertigen kann. Damit dieses Problem deutlich herauskommt, muß die Passage in bezug auf Sprache und argumentative Struktur sehr genau analysiert werden. Zu Beginn wird der Monolog von Kassette vorgespielt.

2. Unterrichtsschritt:
Brutus' Entscheidung (II.1.44–58)

Diese Szene ist bereits in der vorhergehenden Stunde, unter einem anderen Blickwinkel, betrachtet worden. Hier sollte lediglich noch ergänzend herausgearbeitet werden, daß Brutus' Entscheidung an eine wesentliche Bedingung („if the redress will follow") geknüpft ist.

3. Unterrichtsschritt:
Brutus' Alpträume

Anhand der letzten beiden Monologe (II.1.61–69, 77–85) werden Brutus' emotionale Verfassung und seine bei ihm eigentlich überraschende Bereitschaft zur Verstellung (vgl. aber schon II.1.30) herausgearbeitet. Beide Monologe werden zunächst von Kassette vorgespielt und dann in einem arbeitsteiligen Arbeitsauftrag (Gruppe I: 61–69, Gruppe II: 77–85) unter den gleichen Fragestellungen betrachtet.

4. Unterrichtsschritt:
Zusammenfassung der erarbeiteten Ergebnisse

Zum Abschluß werden die Ergebnisse zu den einzelnen Monologen in einem Tafelanschrieb zusammengefaßt.

Hausaufgabe

Hauptgegenstand der folgenden Stunde ist Brutus' Verhalten beim Treffen der Verschwörer (II.1.86–190). Die Passage soll zu Hause vor allem im Hinblick auf Brutus' zwei Ansprachen vorbereitet werden: Wie füllt Brutus seine Führungsrolle aus? Wie läßt sich Brutus' fatale Fehlentscheidung erklären?

1. Zusatzstunde zur 10. Stunde: Vergleich zweier Entscheidungsmonologe (JC II.1.10–85 und Macbeth I.7.1–31)

Bei einer guten Klasse bietet sich die Gelegenheit, die Schüler mit einem weiteren großen Monolog Shakespeares bekannt zu machen und ihnen gleichzeitig eine der bekanntesten Tragödien Shakespeares nahezubringen.

1. Schritt:
Einführung in „Macbeth"

Zu Beginn der Stunde wird die Story der Tragödie referiert, damit die Schüler den Hintergrund des Monologs kennen.

2. Schritt:
Erarbeitung des Macbeth-Monologs

Die Textstelle (vgl. Zusatztext zur 10. Stunde) ist von den Schülern zu Hause sprachlich vorbereitet worden. Zunächst wird der Monolog von Kassette vorgespielt und dann, der inhaltlichen Gliederung der Textstelle folgend, in drei Teilschritten (1–12, 12–25, 25–28) sprachlich und inhaltlich erarbeitet:
1. Macbeth erkennt, daß eine Bluttat unweigerlich entsprechende Konsequenzen nach sich zieht (sowohl im irdischen Leben als auch danach). Diese eher allgemeinen Überlegungen gehen dann, über die Gelenkstelle „poisoned chalice", in eine ethisch-moralische Betrachtung des konkreten Falles über.
2. Die geplante Ermordung Duncans ist für Macbeth aus vier Gründen verwerflich: Duncan ist sein Verwandter, sein König, sein Gast und zudem ein guter Mensch und König. Das letzte Argument zählt für Macbeth am meisten, wie die folgende Bildhäufung zeigt.

3. Von der Betrachtung des Opfers wendet sich Macbeth zum Schluß der Betrachtung des Täters zu und erkennt, daß sein einziges Motiv überbordender Ehrgeiz („vaulting ambition" ist).

Zum Abschluß dieses Schritts sollte der Lehrer noch darauf hinweisen, daß Macbeths Fazit aus diesen Überlegungen zunächst der Verzicht auf den Mord ist („We will proceed no further in this business", 31), daß er aber später von Lady Macbeth mit zweifelhaften, Cassius' würdigen, persuasiven Manipulationen wieder umgestimmt wird.

3. Schritt:
Vergleich der Monologe

Der Vergleich sollte vor allem folgende Punkte herausarbeiten:
– Hauptsächliche Gemeinsamkeit: beide Figuren stehen kurz vor der Entscheidung zu einem Mord und suchen, die geplante Tat zu rechtfertigen.
– Beide verabscheuen eigentlich Gewalttaten.
– Gegensätzliche Motive: „ambition" vs. „general good"
– Unterschiedliche Problemsituation: Bei Macbeth geht es in erster Linie um ethisch-moralische Probleme. Der Monolog führt ihn zu der klaren Erkenntnis, daß die geplante Tat absolut unmoralisch ist, weil Duncan, das Opfer, völlig unschuldig ist. Für Brutus dagegen geht es in erster Linie um ein juristisches Problem, nämlich um die Frage, ob Cäsar schuldig, d. h. ein zukünftiger Tyrann ist. Wenn Cäsar schuldig ist, ist die Tat für Brutus notwendig für das Allgemeinwohl und deshalb ethisch gerechtfertigt. Der potentielle moralische Konflikt – persönliche Freundschaft vs. abstraktes Allgemeinwohl – spielt in Brutus' Monologen keine gewichtige Rolle.

2. Zusatzstunde zur 10. Stunde: Übersetzungsvergleich

Didaktische Vorbemerkungen

Ziel dieser Stunde ist es, anhand eines Übersetzungsvergleichs zu zeigen, daß Übersetzung immer zugleich auch Interpretation ist. Textbasis für diese Stunde sind drei Übersetzungen (von Rothe, Fried [vgl. Worksheet No. 1] und Flatter [vgl. Worksheet No. 2]) des in der 10. Stunde besprochenen 1. Monologs von Brutus (II.1.10–30). Als Referenzübersetzung wird die Prosaübersetzung von Klose (vgl. Worksheet No. 2) hinzugenommen. Schwerpunktmäßig werden folgende Passagen betrachtet: Vers 1–4, 9–12, 18–22. Der Monolog wurde ausgewählt, weil er zentral für die Interpretation der Brutus-Figur ist. Leitfrage der Behandlung ist: In welchem Ausmaß glaubt Brutus an seine eigene Argumentation? Von der Antwort hängen die moralische Integrität und der moralische Anspruch von Brutus ab. Entscheidend für diese Frage sind vor allem die Verse 18–22.

Zur Vorbereitung der Stunde sollen sich die Schüler an den Schwerpunktpassagen selbst zu Hause schriftlich versuchen. Im Unterricht wird zunächst die Übersetzung eines Schülers vorgetragen und kurz besprochen. Anschließend werden die Worksheets mit den professionellen Übersetzungen ausgeteilt und besprochen.

Hinweis: Sehr ausführliche Vorschläge zu einem solchen Übersetzungsvergleich finden sich in dem in der Einleitung vorgestellten Band „Shakespeares ‚Julius Caesar'" von Klaus Busacker. Busacker berücksichtigt insgesamt 10 verschiedene Übersetzungen des Monologs (vgl. S. 473–488) und behandelt diese wesentlich ausführlicher (vgl. S. 287–346) als hier vorgesehen.

Inhaltliche Hinweise zu den Übersetzungen

Vers 1: Brutus bei Rothe sehr zögerlich, an Hamlet erinnernd.

Vers 2: Das aggressive „to spurn" nur bei Fried richtig wiedergegeben. „Ihm bös zu sein" bei Flatter ist läppisch.

Vers 3: Rothes Formulierung „der Staat allein hat Grund" erweckt den Eindruck, als habe der Staat andere Gründe als Brutus, die dieser aus Staatsfrömmigkeit übernehmen will. Was gemeint ist, wird bei Fried am deutlichsten.

Vers 4: Das Präsens bei Rothe zeigt den spekulativen Charakter von Brutus' Reflexionen weniger deutlich als die anderen beiden Übersetzungen.

Vers 9: Flatters „Der Fluch der Größe ist's…" impliziert, daß Größe *immer* zu Verantwortungslosigkeit führt.

Vers 11: Bei Rothe fehlt Brutus' Einschränkung auf seine eigenen Erkenntnisse und Erfahrungen.

Vers 18–22: Bei *Rothe* erscheint Cäsars Ehrgeiz als vage Möglichkeit: „Vielleicht daß Cäsar genauso fühlt" (18/19). „Fühlen" ist hier im übrigen deplaziert – es geht um Cäsars mögliches Verhalten in der Zukunft. Ebensowenig geht es um Cäsars „Wesen" (20), sondern darum, welche tatsächlichen Verdachtsmomente gegen ihn vorzubringen sind. Insgesamt erscheint hier Brutus' Argumentation am wenigsten überzeugend für den Leser und für Brutus selbst. Am Anfang erscheint Brutus sehr zögerlich, am Ende denkt er rein manipulativ, *gegen* seine eigenen moralischen Zweifel.

MACBETH ACT ONE SCENE VII

Macbeth

    If it were done when 'tis done, then 'twere well
    It were done quickly. If th' assassination
    Could trammel up the consequence, and catch,
    With his surcease, success; that but this blow
5 Might be the be-all and the end-all here –
    But here upon this bank and shoal of time –
    We'd jump life to come. But in these cases
    We still have judgment here, that we but teach
    Bloody instructions, which being taught return
10 To plague th' inventor. This even-handed justice
    Commends th' ingredience of our poison'd chalice
    To our own lips. He's here in double trust:
    First, as I am his kinsman and his subject –
    Strong both against the deed; then, as his host,
15 Who should against his murderer shut the door,
    Not bear the knife myself. Besides, this Duncan
    Hath borne his faculties so meek, hath been
    So clear in his great office, that his virtues
    Will plead like angels, trumpet-tongu'd, against
20 The deep damnation of his taking-off;
    And pity, like a naked new-born babe,
    Striding the blast, or heaven's cherubin hors'd
    Upon the sightless couriers of the air,
    Shall blow the horrid deed in every eye,
25 That tears shall drown the wind. I have no spur
    To prick the sides of my intent, but only
    Vaulting ambition, which o'er-leaps itself,
    And falls on th' other.

Aus: *The Alexander Shakespeare,* Macbeth. Collins/Klett, Stuttgart 1986,
S. 59–61.

1–28   This speech has often been regarded as one of the
great Shakespearian 'set-piece' soliloquies (remember that Shakespeare uses such speeches to
give his characters the opportunity for self-revela-
tion). Macbeth begins uneasily arguing with himself, perhaps almost muttering, but later he becomes deeply moved and eloquent. It is useful, and
often satisfying, to try speeches out for oneself.

1   The first *done* means 'over and done with'.

2–3   *If th'assassination ... consequence:* if the murder could be completely decisive and without unpleasant results.
trammel: entangle in a net.

4   *surcease:* death.

5   *here:* on earth.

6   *this bank and shoal of time:* Macbeth seems to view human life as a sandbank in eternity. Many of his actions do seem to be based on the idea that he is in a predicament like a shipwreck.

7   *We'd jump the life to come:* I'd risk what comes after death.

8–10   Macbeth is worried that a bloody act often provokes bloody retaliation.

10–12   *This even-handed justice ... lips:* Impartial justice rules that we should drink the poison we administer to another.

12–28   Macbeth now speaks with real emotion, and in doing so reveals a genuine respect for Duncan's goodness, and also a respect for decent human values. He knows, clearly, that what he is thinking of doing is evil.

12–16   The *double trust* is *(a)* the combined relationship of being a relative and a subject, and *(b)* being the king's host.

17   *Hath borne ... meek:* Has used his authority as king with such genuine humility.

18   *clear:* innocent.

20   *taking-off:* murder.

21–5   The two pictures, of the baby and the *cherubin,* would not have seemed as similar to Shakespeare's audience as they do to us. Cherubs were not chubby babies but senior angels. But both baby and angels are riding the winds (*blast* and *sigthless couriers* or invisible runners) and they are all, in Macbeth's vivid imagination, going to make the crime known to all (*blow the horrid deed in every eye*).

27–8   Jumping directly into one's saddle was a young man's way of showing-off. Possibly Shakespeare means 'overhoots and falls to the ground on the other side' by the last few words. Or it could mean simply that the rider, having cleared an obstacle, falls off his horse on the other side of it. In any case it is clear that Macbeth now knows that this ambition is an evil one.

Flatter ist in dieser Passage obskur: Was heißt „trifft" (18), wer oder was ist „er" in Vers 20 und in Vers 21? Vor allem fehlt der in „may" zum Ausdruck kommende Zweifel von Brutus, wenn Flatter übersetzt: „Das trifft auch Cäsar" (18; vgl. 19). *Fried* übersetzt hier z. T. in sehr schlechtem Deutsch: „Drum hindern, eh er's kann!" (19); vgl. auch „grell" (20). Die Übersetzung „Mißstand" (19) für „quarell" impliziert eine Sachaussage über die Situation in Rom (dort herrscht ein Mißstand), nicht über eine bestimmte Rechtslage oder Argumentationssituation. In der Übersetzung von „fashion" mit „beweist" (21) fehlt das Element des Manipulierens, das in Flatters „stellt es so dar" deutlicher wird.

Dazu ist vielleicht ein Blick auf die Vielfalt der Bedeutungen des Wortes „to fashion" ganz hilfreich: T. S. Dorsch paraphrasiert in der Arden Edition „fashion it thus" als „make it look like this, put it that way". Das Shorter Oxford English Dictionary (SOED) gibt folgende Bedeutungen:

1. "to give fashion or shape to"; "to form, mould, shape"
2. a) „to frame, make (rare)", 1549;
   b) "to contrive, manage", 1604;
3. "to change the fashion of; to transform" (obsolet) – 1753; "to counterfeit, pervert" (obs.), SHAKESPEARE.
4. "To accomodate, to adopt to"

Obwohl alle drei besprochenen Übersetzungen sehr bekannt sind, enthalten sie doch selbst in diesem kurzen Stück Fehler oder schlechtes Deutsch. Damit die Schüler die Probleme der Übersetzer besser verstehen, sollte man darauf hinweisen, daß diese Übersetzer das Versschema möglichst getreu wiedergeben wollten. Dies ist gerade beim Englischen sehr schwer, weil es viel mehr einsilbige Wörter als das Deutsche aufweist.

Vergleich der Übersetzungen in bezug auf die Leitfrage: Bei *Rothe* handelt Brutus eindeutig gegen seine eigene Überzeugung (Cäsars „Wesen" gäbe keinen Anlaß zum Handeln). Am stärksten ist Brutus bei *Flatter* von seiner Argumentation überzeugt („Das trifft auch Cäsar", Vers 18, nicht: „Das könnte auch . . ."). Auch in der Übersetzung von *Fried* ist Brutus stärker als bei Rothe von seiner Argumentation überzeugt – allerdings nicht so deutlich wie bei Flatter.

Worksheet No. 1 (Übersetzungsbeispiele zu W. Shakespeare: Julius Caesar, II.1)

Übersetzer: Hans Rothe

Nur wenn er stirbt, nur dann – – und dabei habe
ich selbst nicht Grund, mich gegen in zu kehren,
der Staat allein hat Grund. – Er will die Krone:
wie sehr sie ihn verändert, darum gehts.
5 Nur wenn die Sonne wärmt, zeigt sich die Natter,
und dann erst braucht man Vorsicht. Ihm die Krone –
das heißt der Schlange ihren Giftzahn schenken
damit sie nach Belieben Böses tut.
Mißbrauch wird Größe, wenn sich das Gewissen
10 trennt von der Macht – nein, ich will gerecht sein:
nie hat sich Caesar mehr von Leidenschaft
als von Vernunft beherrschen lassen. Aber
wer weiß nicht daß der Ehrgeiz über Demut
zu klimmen pflegt? der Demut gilt sein Blick,
15 an sie ist er geklammert. Kaum ist er oben,
zeigt er der Demutsleiter seinen Rücken,
sieht in die Wolken, mißachtet die Stufen
die ihn emporgeführt. Vielleicht daß Caesar
genau so fühlt. Dann komme man ihm zuvor.
20 Doch durch sein Wesen wäre nicht bedingt
daß man ihn angreift. Anders muß mans wenden:
wenn ihm mehr Macht wird, weckt es ihm den Macht-
                                 rausch,
und deshalb gleicht er einem Schlangenei, –
25 das erst erbrütet Unheil wirken kann, –
doch in der Schale kann man es zertreten.

Rothe, Hans: *Der elisabethanische Shakespeare.* Bd. 6. München/
Wien: Langen-Müller 1963, p. 33f.

Übersetzer: Erich Fried

Es *muß* durch seinen Tod sein: ich für *mein* Teil
Hab keinen Grund, den Stoß ihm zu versetzen,
Als das gemeine Wohl. Er will die Krone.
Wie die ihn ändern würde, ist die Frage.
5 Der schöne Tag ja weckt die giftge Schlange,
Drum Vorsicht, wie man geht. – Ihn krönen? – das;
Und dann – gewiß, wir setzen ihm den Zahn ein,
Mit dem er Schaden tun kann, wenn er will.
Die Größe führt zu Mißbrauch, wo sie *Macht*
10 Abtrennt vom Mitgefühl. Nun sah ich Caesar
In Wahrheit vom Gefühl nie *mehr* beherrscht
Als von Vernunft. Doch oft erwies sich schon
Die Demut als der jungen Herrschsucht Leiter:
Der da hinaufsteigt, neigt ihr sein Gesicht zu,
15 Doch kaum erreicht er ihre höchste Sprosse,
Kehrt er der Leiter gleich den Rücken zu,
Blickt in die Wolken, schmäht die niederen Tritte,
Die ihn hinaufgebracht. – Das kann auch Caesar;
Drum hindern, *eh* er's kann! – Und weil dem Mißstand
20 Noch nicht grell anzusehen ist, wie er sein wird,
Beweist es so: Das, was er ist, vergrößert,
Wüchs jetzt schon da und dort zum Äußersten!
Und darum denkt ihn euch als Ei der Schlange,
Die, wenn sie auskriecht, giftig werden *müßte*,
25 Und schlagt ihn in der Schale tot.

Aus: Fried, Erich: *Shakespeare-Übersetzungen: Romeo und Julia,
Julius Caesar, Hamlet.* München: Hanser 1968, p. 119f.

Übersetzer: Dietrich Klose

Es muß durch seinen Tod sein; aber ich für meinen Teil
habe keinen persönlichen Grund, gegen ihn loszugehen –
außer für das Gemeinwohl. Er möchte gern gekrönt werden.
Wie dies sein Wesen verändern könnte, da liegt die Frage.
5 Der helle Tag ist es, der die Natter hervorbringt und
aufmerksames Gehen erfordert. Ihn krönen? – Das (daß) –
ich gebe es zu, setzen wir ihm einen Stachel ein, mit
dem er nach seinem Belieben Gefahren heraufbeschwören
kann. Mißbrauch von Größe liegt vor, wenn Macht von Mit-
10 leid [besser: Gewissen] getrennt wird. Und um die Wahrheit von Caesar zu sagen: Ich habe nicht gehört, daß seine Leidenschaften ihn jemals stärker beherrscht hätten
als seine Vernunft. Aber es ist eine allgemeine Erkenntnis, daß bescheidenes Auftreten des jungen Ehrgeizes
15 Leiter ist, der der Emporkletternde sein Gesicht zuwendet. Aber wenn er einmal die höchste Sprosse erreicht
hat, dann wendet er der Leiter den Rücken, schaut in die
Wolken und verachtet die niedrigen Stufen, mit deren
Hilfe er emporstieg. Das könnte auch Caesar; damit er
20 es aber nicht vermag, beuge vor. Und da die Anklage, gemessen daran, was Caesar *ist*, nicht stichhaltig ist,
betrachte es folgendermaßen: Erhöhte sich seine Stellung
noch weiter, so würde das zu diesen und jenen Auswüchsen
führen. Und deshalb betrachte ihn als ein Schlangenei,
25 das – erst einmal ausgebrütet – seiner Natur nach wohl
zum Unheil heranwächst, und töte ihn in der Schale.

Aus: Klose, Dietrich: *William Shakespeare: Julius Caesar.* Stuttgart:
Reclam 1976, p. 43.

Übersetzer: Richard Flatter

Es muß durch seinen Tod sein. Ich, persönlich,
Hab keine Ursache, ihm bös zu sein;
Das Wohl des Staates ist's. Er will gekrönt sein.
Wie ihn das ändern mag – das ist die Frage.
5 Wenn der Tag warm ist, regen sich die Schlangen;
Da heißt's, vorsichtig gehn. Ihn krönen – freilich –
Der Schlange auch noch einen Stachel geben!
Daß seine Willkür uns gefährlich wird!
Der Fluch der Größe ist's, daß ihre Macht
10 Sich vom Gewissen lossagt. Zwar, in Wahrheit –:
Ich weiß von keinem Fall, wo Caesars Ehrsucht
Ihm die Vernunft nahm; doch Erfahrung lehrt,
Die Demut ist die Leiter junger Machtgier,
An die sich sorgsam hält, wer aufwärts klettert;
15 Doch hat er erst den höchsten Tritt erreicht,
Dreht er der Leiter achtlos seinen Rücken,
Blickt in die Wolken und verhöhnt die Sprossen,
Die ihn hinaufgebracht. Das trifft auch Caesar;
Drum, eh' er's trifft, seht vor. Doch da der Rechtsfall
20 Sich nicht auf das aufbaun läßt, was er *ist*,
Stellt es so dar: das, was er ist, vergrößert,
Müßte zu dem und dem Verhängnis führen.
Denkt von ihm so wie von dem Ei der Schlange:
Erst einmal ausgeschlüpft, braucht sie ihr Gift;
25 Man muß sie vorher töten!

Flatter, Richard: *Shakespeare. Bd. III.* Wien: Walter Krieg: 1954,
p. 273f.

11. Stunde: Vorbereitung und Durchführung des Attentats

Didaktische Vorbemerkungen

Mit dem ersten (und einzigen) Treffen der Verschwörer ist die Verschwörung nicht mehr eine Möglichkeit unter anderen, sondern ein Faktum. Es geht jetzt vor allem darum, erfolgreich zu planen und zu handeln, um so das Ziel, die Befreiung Roms vom Tyrannen Cäsar, zu erreichen. Damit tritt neben die moralische Qualität die Handlungskompetenz als zweiter wichtiger Maßstab zur Beurteilung der Figuren. Im Mittelpunkt dieser Stunde steht daher die Frage, wie sich Brutus angesichts dieser Situation verhält. Insofern stellt diese Stunde eine Fortsetzung der vorausgehenden dar.

Die Stunde beginnt mit einer Analyse von Brutus' Ansprache an die Mitverschwörer. Im zweiten und gewichtigsten Teil der Stunde sollte vor allem herausgearbeitet werden, daß Brutus' metaphernreiche Argumentation gegen die Ermordung von Antonius Ausdruck seiner inneren Gespaltenheit ist, wegen der die Verschwörung eigentlich von Anfang an zum Scheitern verurteilt ist. Die Stunde schließt mit einer kurzen Betrachtung der Mordszene und des chaotischen Verhaltens der Verschwörer direkt nach der Tat.

Notes on interpretation

With the first (and only) meeting of the conspirators the idea of a conspiracy becomes irrevocable reality. Therefore, it is surprising how firmly Brutus claims authority from the very beginning and is granted it by his fellow conspirators, even by Cassius, who should have known (and knows) better. Brutus establishes his claim for leadership by formulating, as it were, the "ideology" of their conspiracy (II.1.114–140). At first, Brutus describes the present situation ("high-sighted tyranny") which is the reason and justification for the conspiracy, then he tries to motivate his friends ("insuppressive mettle of our spirits") and establishes a high moral claim for their intention ("to redress", "even virtue of our enterprise"). On the whole, Brutus gives his fellow conspirators the feeling of outstanding moral superiority which can easily do without formal obligations like oaths.

This ist the first example of Brutus asserting himself against Cassius. The second, more important question of Cicero's participation is decided by Brutus against all the other conspirators (141–154). The drama offers no criteria with which to judge the quality of this decision. But the third example of Brutus' self-assertion, the question of the future treatment of Antony, is crucial to the success of the whole conspiracy, and the further development of the action clearly shows that Brutus' decision to spare Antony is a fatal mistake.

Brutus gives three reasons for his decision:
– Antony is mainly given to sensual pleasures and therefore harmless. Cf. Caesar on Antony in I.2.205.
– Antony is only Caesar's underling without independent initiative.
– The public would not accept two murders.

These arguments are rational in that they can be discussed and proved or disproved by further (or later) evidence. But the core of Brutus' opposition to Antony's murder is of an ideological nature and reflects his inner conflict.

Although Brutus realizes that "Caesar must bleed" (171), he still laments that it is impossible to "come by Caesar's spirit and not dismember Caesar" (169/170). Brutus gives here the slightly pathetic impression of a man who wants to sleep with a woman without losing his virginity. In order to save his own moral integrity Brutus artificially distinguishes between the "spirit of Caesar" ("there is no blood") and the "man", and between "sacrificers" resp. "purgers" (who very aesthetically dispose of bloodless spirits) and "butchers" resp. "murderers" (who shed real blood by killing real bodies). Brutus' metaphorical appeal "to carve him as a dish for the gods" is as embarrassing as his later order "Let us bathe our hands in Caesar's blood up to the elbows, and besmear our swords" (III.1.107/108), which is for Brutus no doubt part of his ritual of "sacrificing Caesar", but for other people just an act of disgusting barbarism.

In the end, Brutus' opposition to Antony's murder is not based on rational arguments but on an irrational chain of metaphorical associations of the following nature: Antony is a "limb" of Caesar — only "butchers" hack limbs off — we are not "butchers" but "purgers" — therefore, Antony (the "limb") is to be spared.

By ritualizing and thus aestheticizing the assassination, Brutus tries to repress the simple truth, that an assassination always implies "butchery" in some way, no matter how honourable the murderers' (or, the "sacrificers'") motives may be. Ironically, it is Antony who abuses the conspirators later as "butchers" in his monologue (III.1.256). Because Brutus cannot face the unavoidable loss of his moral integrity, he takes the wrong decision (i.e. to spare Antony) and thus loses the game before it has really begun.

In the end, Brutus fails *in spite of* his good intentions and this failure is tragic because he fails *on account of* his good intentions. To be sure, Cassius would have managed the situation much better, but on account of his doubtful morale we would not hope as much for his success as we do for Brutus'.

JC is not a psychological drama and Brutus' problems therefore are not its end, but a literary device representing the general dilemma of all revolutions, namely the unavoidable contradiction of means and ends.

P.S.: Note the ironical ambivalence of lines 112–118: They could refer not only to the conspirators' but also to the author's perennial success!

Verlauf der Stunde

1. Unterrichtsschritt:
„oath" vs. „honesty" (II.1.86–140)

Im Mittelpunkt des ersten Teils der Stunde steht Brutus' Ansprache an die Verschwörer. Die Analyse der Textstelle (114–140) sollte unter zwei Fragestellungen vollzogen werden:
– Wie ist die Ansprache inhaltlich aufgebaut?
– Welche „ideologische" Funktion hat sie?

Zum Abschluß dieses Schritts wird die Ansprache von Kassette vorgespielt und die der Rezitation zugrundeliegende Interpretation mit der im Unterricht erarbeiteten verglichen.

2. Unterrichtsschritt:
„sacrificers" vs. „butchers" (II.1.141–190)

Zunächst gilt es, an drei Beispielen (oath?, Cicero?, Antony?) zu zeigen, daß Brutus von allen als Führer akzeptiert wird und er damit letztendlich entscheidet (und verantworten muß), was getan wird.

Im Mittelpunkt steht jedoch die Analyse von Brutus' Argumentation gegen die von Cassius vorgeschlagene Ermordung von Antonius. Zunächst wird die antinomische Grundstruktur der Rede als Gegenüberstellung zweier Bild- und Begriffskomplexe (vgl. Tafelanschrieb) herausgearbeitet und als Ausdruck von Brutus' innerer Gespaltenheit interpretiert. Im Anschluß daran werden die Argumente für bzw. gegen die Ermordung von Antonius kritisch überprüft.

3. Unterrichtsschritt:
Cäsars Ermordung (III.1.1–120)

Unter Rückgriff auf die 7./8. Stunde („Charakter" Cäsars) werden zunächst folgende Punkte rekapituliert bzw. neu erarbeitet:
- Cäsar wird ermordet, als seine Arroganz einen unerträglichen Höhepunkt erreicht hat.
- Cäsars letzte Worte lassen ihn dann nicht nur wesentlich sympathischer erscheinen, sondern implizieren auch erhebliche Kritik an Brutus' moralischer Selbstgerechtigkeit.
- Der Rest des Dramas ist von Antonius' ausschließlich positivem Cäsarbild bestimmt.

Zum Abschluß der Stunde wird das Verhalten der Verschwörer nach dem Mord betrachtet: Wichtig sind dabei die folgenden Punkte:
- Die Verschwörer reagieren ziemlich planlos.
- Brutus ordnet eine abstoßende rituelle Handlung an.

Hausaufgabe

In der folgenden Stunde wird die Begegnung zwischen Brutus und Antonius (III.1.124–274) besprochen. Die Schüler sollen die Textstelle sprachlich und inhaltlich zu Hause vorbereiten und das Worksheet ausfüllen. Auf diese Weise wird die häusliche Vorbereitung im Hinblick auf die Ziele der folgenden Stunde hin strukturiert. Das Worksheet ist in Form einer „Charakterisierungsmatrix" angelegt, aus der sich leicht ablesen läßt, wer wen wie beurteilt. In der waagrechten Kopfleiste sind, als „target figures", die Figuren aufgetragen, *über* die etwas ausgesagt wird, in der senkrechten Spalte sind, unter „perspective", die Figuren aufgetragen, die das entsprechende Urteil abgeben. Das Worksheet wird am Ende der Stunde ausgeteilt, wenn die Hausaufgabe gegeben wird.

Target figure / Point of view	Brutus	Antony	Caesar	Cassius
Conclusions from behaviour				
Brutus				
Antony — Dialogue / Monologue				
Cassius				
Summary				

12. Stunde:
Antonius als Gegenspieler von Brutus

Didaktische Vorbemerkungen

Die Begegnung von Brutus und Antonius in III.1. ist eine Schlüsselstelle dieses Dramas von sehr komplexer Bedeutungsvielfalt (vgl. Notes on interpretation), die im Unterricht nicht erschöpfend behandelt werden kann. Diese Szene markiert nicht nur einen entscheidenden Höhepunkt der Handlung, sondern auch einen Wendepunkt in der zentralen Perspektive des Dramas, die bisher fast ausschließlich von Brutus bestimmt wurde: Antonius' engagierte und bedingungslose Parteinahme für Cäsar zwingt den Leser/Zuschauer, seine bisherigen Vorstellungen von Brutus und Cäsar in Frage zu stellen. Auf der Bildebene wird dieser Perspektivenwechsel unterstrichen durch die modifizierte Wiederaufnahme des von Brutus thematisierten Gegensatzpaares „sacrificers" vs. „butchers" in dem diese Szene dominierenden Blut-Motiv.

Brutus und Antonius repräsentieren nicht nur gegensätzliche Meinungen über Cäsar, sondern auch gegensätzliche Charaktere: Brutus ist aufrichtig, altruistisch (vgl. seine Besorgnis um „the general good") und rational, Antonius dagegen verschlagen – hierin gleicht er Cassius –, egoistisch (vgl. seine verantwortungslose Rachsucht) und emotional (vgl. seine echte Trauer um Cäsar). Dieser Gegensatz zwischen den beiden Figuren erfährt eine zusätzliche dramatische Ausgestaltung in dem unterschiedlichen Charakter der beiden Forumsreden (III.2).

Die Schwierigkeit dieser Stunde besteht darin, daß die Schüler eine relativ große Textmenge überblicken müssen, weil die o.g. Problemstellungen nur schwer durch eine sukzessive Behandlung des Textes erarbeitet werden können.

Die Begegnung zwischen Brutus und Antonius wird in fünf Unterrichtsschritten behandelt. Zunächst wird die allgemeine Bedeutung der Begegnung für den weiteren Verlauf des Dramas herausgearbeitet. In den folgenden drei Unterrichtsschritten wird die Begegnung jeweils im Hinblick auf eine Figur (Reihenfolge: Brutus, Cäsar, Antonius) untersucht. Jeder dieser Schritte wird von einem kurzen „Experten"-Vortrag eines Schülers (vgl. Hausaufgabe zu dieser Stunde) eingeleitet, der dann im Unterrichtsgespräch diskutiert wird. Der weitere Verlauf und der Einsatz der im Stundenblatt vorgeschlagenen Impulse ist abhängig von Inhalt und Qualität des Expertenvortrags. Zum Abschluß der Stunde wird die Funktion der die ganze Szene durchziehenden „imagery of blood and destruction" untersucht.

Notes on interpretation

Though being almost squeezed between the two dramatic highlights of JC (i.e. Caesar's murder and the forum scene), the meeting between Brutus and Antony in III.1.124–274 is the drama's real turning point, and that in two important respects:
– After Brutus' decision to let Antony speak in the forum the conspiracy is finally doomed to fail.
– Our hitherto mainly negative picture of Caesar is seriously questioned by Antony's genuine admiration for Caesar. This, in turn, also questions Brutus' justification for his murder of Caesar.

The following more detailed analysis of the scene and its main figures will show other important aspects of the meeting between Brutus and Antony.

In retrospect, it is obvious that the conspiracy against Caesar mainly failed because Brutus did not also murder Antony. To his fellow conspirators, Brutus gave two reasons for sparing Antony:
- Antony is harmless because he lacks self-determination ("but a limb of Caesar") and because he is effeminated ("given to diverse pleasures"). Both judgements were wrong as this scene and the further development of the action show. Apparently, Brutus' practical psychology is faulty.
- Brutus also wanted to spare Antony because he abhores bloodshed (cf. "butcher" vs. "sacrificer") and because he did not want to appear in the eyes of the public as a "butcher". In both respects, Brutus fails: He ist publicly accused by Antony of being a "butcher" (cf. III.2.) and the murder of Caesar results in a terrible civil war. Thus, Brutus' attempt at divorcing questionable means (murder) from honourable ends (abolition of tyranny) has failed in the end, too. The pervading imagery of blood and destruction underlines this failure.

But Brutus' failure is even more complex. His certainty of winning Antony as a friend or at least as a supporter rests on two questionable presuppositions. The first is that Caesar is really the cause of the "general wrong of Rome" (171), resp. that there is something wrong at all in Rome. Remember that Antony twice demands (132–134 and 222/223) a satisfying explanation. Brutus, feeling sure of his cause, accepts this demand ("Or else were this a savage spectacle", 224) but never really fulfills it. This assumption is questioned in two ways:
- By Brutus himself in his first monologue (II.1.10–34): "Let's fashion it thus" (cf. lesson 10). Brutus' lack of substantial evidence for Caesar's dangerousness and ambition is later on rhetorically exposed by Antony in his forum speech.
- By Antony's genuine admiration for Caesar.

Brutus' second implicit assumption is that rational values are more important for everyone than private emotional loyalties: "Our reasons are so full of good regard that were you, Antony, the son of Caesar, you would be satisfied" (225–227). To Antony, full of deeply felt sorrow about Caesar's death, this must appear as wilful and detestable cynicism. Apparently, Brutus is not only incapable of strong emotions himself (to have killed his "best lover", III.2.46, has never been a serious problem for him), but is also not capable of imagining strong emotions in other people. Only compare Brutus' well-set phrasings ("And pity to the general wrong of Rome, *as fire drives out fire, so pity pity,* hath done this deed to Caesar", 171–174; cf. also III.2.25–27) with Antony's uncontrolled (and in the given situation dangerous) outburst of sorrow in front of the conspirators (195–211) and his irresponsible and egotistic readiness to turn the whole world into suffering and chaos, only to compensate for the deep violation of his feelings.

This does not mean that Antony is morally superior to Brutus – on the contrary, he proves here and later to be a skilful contriver, a revengeful egoist, and a ruthless and efficient executer (cf. IV.1). Nevertheless, Antony represents with his intense emotionality an important antithesis to Brutus' subdued rationality. Brutus we would respect, Antony we would love or hate. On a more abstract level, Brutus represents a personally disinterested political view on life, while Antony embodies the viewpoint of the private individual.

The question whether Caesar "really" was ambitious and thus a future tyrant is the pivot of the whole drama. Up to the meeting between Brutus and Antony, Caesar was mainly presented as a negative figure, not only by the conspirators but also by his arrogant "live performances" on the stage. With the introduction of Antony as a fervent admirer of Caesar, this hitherto negative image of Caesar is seriously questioned and we remember his deep disappointment at Brutus' final disloyalty ("Et tu Brutus?' – Then fall, Caesar!", III.1.77) and Brutus' rather awkward attempts at convincing himself of Caesar's dangerous ambition (II.1.10–34). Certainly, Caesar is nowhere in the drama presented as an agreeable person, but that is really not a sufficient justification for his assassination.

In the end, the drama offers no definite clues to the question of whether Caesar is a potential tyrant or not. Nor do historical studies of Elizabethan opinions on Caesar provide much help either – they are as ambivalent as the evidence in the drama itself. Thus, the reader/spectator has to decide for himself, whether Caesar is to represent a potential tyrant or not, which necessarily implies a decision on the question of whether Brutus is a "sacrificer" or a "butcher" (perhaps not by intention but by effect). Alternatively, the reader may come to the conclusion that in JC Shakespeare tried among other things to show that it is impossible to know the "truth" about a person.

Verlauf der Stunde

1. Unterrichtsschritt:
Die Bedeutung der Begegnung
(III.1.124–274)

Neben der allgemeinen Bedeutung dieser Begegnung (Einführung des Gegenspielers und Vorbereitung des Wendepunktes der Handlung in III.2) sollten auch die jeweilige Situation, Ziele und Handlungsmöglichkeiten der beiden Figuren vor der Begegnung genauer betrachtet werden: Brutus hat hier die letzte Chance, sich eines gefährlichen Rivalen zu entledigen, Antonius auf der anderen Seite muß sich überlegen, mit welcher Taktik er sein Ziel, eine öffentliche Grabrede halten zu können, am erfolgreichsten erreichen kann.

2. Unterrichtsschritt:
Brutus: „sacrificer" oder „butcher"?
(III.1.165–173 und 224–227)

Wichtig ist, daß die Schüler erkennen, daß durch Antonius Brutus' moralische Integrität ernsthaft in Frage gestellt wird. Dies wird deutlicher, wenn auf II.1.162–183 (vgl. 10. Stunde) zurückgegriffen wird („Let's be sacrificers, but not butchers"). In der vorliegenden Szene tritt dieser Gegensatz in verwandelter Form als Gegenüberstellung von „bloody hands" und „pitiful hearts" (165–173) auf. Ggf. sollte diese Stelle gemeinsam gelesen werden.
Wichtig ist hier auch, daß sich die Schüler die Szene möglichst bildhaft und in ihrer Wirkung auf den Zuschauer (alle Verschwörer sind blutbesudelt!) vorstellen.
Einer der Schüler-Experten für Brutus trägt das Ergebnis seiner Hausarbeit vor, das anschließend diskutiert wird. Die Ergebnisse werden an der Tafel festgehalten.

3. Unterrichtsschritt:
Cäsar: „tyrant" oder „the most noble man"?

Auch hier sind drei verschiedene Perspektiven (Brutus Sicht von Cäsar, Cäsars Verhalten in früheren Szenen, schließlich Antonius' positive Sicht) zu besprechen. Dabei sollte in zweifacher Weise auf Vergangenes, zuvor Besprochenes, zurückgegriffen werden: Einmal auf das im ersten Teil des Dramas präsentierte Bild Cäsars (vgl. 7./8. Stunde), zum anderen auf Brutus' Rechtfertigungsmonolog (II.1.10–34, vgl. 10. Stunde), in dem deutlich wurde, daß Brutus selbst Zweifel an Cäsars tatsächlicher Gefährlichkeit hat. Herausgearbeitet werden sollte nicht nur, daß durch Antonius positive Sicht von Cäsar Brutus' negatives Cäsarbild in Frage gestellt wird, sondern auch, daß von der Beurteilung Cäsars auch wesentlich die Beurteilung von Brutus abhängt („or else were this a savage spectacle", 224) – nicht nur für Antonius, sondern auch für den Zuschauer.

Auch hier steht am Anfang ein kurzer Schülervortrag, der anschließend diskutiert wird.

4. Unterrichtsschritt:
Antonius: ein ehrlicher Heuchler

Anknüpfungspunkt für die Betrachtung von Antonius ist die unterschiedliche Beurteilung von Antonius durch Brutus und Cassius in II.1.165–189 (vgl. 11. Stunde), die in der vorliegenden Szene noch einmal nachdrücklich bekräftigt wird (III.1.144–147 und 231–236). Zum Unglück der Verschwörer setzt sich Brutus auch hier wieder durch.

Im Hinblick auf Antonius sind vor allem drei Aspekte der Szene wichtig:
– Antonius' raffinierte Verstellung (bei gleichzeitiger offener Loyalität gegenüber Cäsar), mit der er seine Ziele erreicht. Die für Antonius' Verhalten in dieser Szene charakteristische Mischung von Offenheit und Verschlagenheit wird für den Zuschauer erst durch Antonius' Monolog voll durchschaubar.
– Antonius Emotionalität und echte Zuneigung zu Cäsar, die nicht nur in seinem Monolog, sondern auch in seinem – für ihn und seine Taktik gefährlichen – Schmerzausbruch (205–211) zum Ausdruck kommt.
– Antonius' zügellose Rachsucht schließlich kommt in seinem Monolog deutlich zum Ausdruck (III.1.255–274).

Nach der Diskussion des Schülervortrags wird Antonius' Monolog von Kassette vorgespielt. Zum Abschluß dieses Unterrichtsschritts werden Brutus und Antonius am Beispiel ihrer Einstellung zu Cäsar, ihrem gemeinsamen Freund, als Vertreter unterschiedlicher Lebenseinstellungen (Brutus: Primat des Politischen, Antonius: Primat der privaten Perspektive) gegenübergestellt.

5. Unterrichtsschritt:
Imagery of blood and destruction

Die ganze Begegnung wird dominiert von Bildern (sprachlich und optisch auf der Bühne!) von Blut („blood" allein 10 x) und Zerstörung bzw. Grausamkeit (gehäuft in Antonius' Monolog). Zunächst werden die wichtigsten Beispiele an der Tafel gesammelt (vgl. Tafelanschrieb), dann werden die möglichen Funktionen dieses Bildkomplexes (düstere Vorausdeutung, Mord gebiert Mord) im Unterrichtsgespräch erarbeitet.

Hausaufgabe

Die Behandlung der beiden Forumsreden (III.2) in der folgenden Doppelstunde erfordert eine gründliche häusliche Vorbereitung. Deshalb sollen die Schüler die Reden nicht nur lesen, sondern auch schriftlich Gliederungsvorschläge und kurze Zusammenfassungen der vorgeschlagenen Abschnitte für beide Reden erarbeiten.

13./14. Stunde:
Techniken der Überredung II:
Die Forumsreden

Didaktische Vorbemerkungen

Die Forumsszene sollte unbedingt in einer Doppelstunde behandelt werden, da die beiden Reden von sehr unterschiedlicher Länge sind und Antonius' Rede bei einer Aufteilung in zwei Einzelstunden zwangsläufig auseinandergerissen würde.

Der Kampf um die Macht nach Cäsars Tod wird in JC mit rhetorischen Mitteln ausgefochten und entschieden. In der Forumsszene kommt es für beide Kontrahenten darauf an, das Volk für sich zu gewinnen. Wie so oft in der Politik entscheiden nicht die Sachargumente – diese werden gar nicht diskutiert –, sondern die Form der öffentlichen Präsentation. Der Hauptunterschied zu modernen Wahlreden liegt darin, daß die öffentliche Präsentation hier nicht von PR-Managern als Mediatoren „gestylt", sondern von den Rednern selbst bestimmt wird und daher als Ausdruck ihrer Persönlichkeit analysiert werden kann.

Damit ergeben sich für die Behandlung der beiden Reden folgende zentrale Fragestellungen:

– Wie sind die beiden Reden inhaltlich und formal aufgebaut? Im Vordergrund stehen sollte dabei die Appellfunktion der Rede, also die Frage, in welcher Weise die Reden auf die tatsächlichen oder vermeintlichen Merkmale der Rezipienten (in diesem Falle der Plebejer) ausgerichtet sind. Maßstab für die Beurteilung der Reden sollte nicht ihre rhetorische Struktur sein, sondern ihr tatsächlicher Erfolg.
– Inwiefern sind die Reden Ausdruck der jeweiligen Rednerpersönlichkeit?
– Worin liegt die weitergehende Bedeutung von Brutus' Niederlage?

Die Doppelstunde beginnt mit der Analyse von Brutus' Rede als Ausdruck seiner rationalen und moralischen Weltsicht. Antonius' Rede wird in vier Schritten behandelt (Überblick, III.2.75–119, 120–162, 171–254). Bevor im sechsten Schritt die beiden Forumsreden gegenübergestellt werden, wird zunächst Antonius' Rede ganz oder in Ausschnitten von Kassette vorgespielt. Zum Abschluß der Stunde werden die unmittelbaren (Raserei des Pöbels in III.3.) und die weiterreichenden Folgen von Antonius' rhetorischem Sieg besprochen.

Notes on interpretation

JC is rather unique in that the battle for power is not decided on the battlefield but in a kind of rhetorical duel.

Ironically, only one of the duellists, Antony, knows that there is going to be a duel, while the other, Brutus, in his rationalistic optimism still believes that only a short explanation is demanded of him. Thus, Brutus is entering a contest, the rules of which are defined later on by his opponent. To be sure, Brutus tries to set the rules himself (cf. III.1.237–252) but does not reckon with the opposition and cleverness of Antony, who makes a sport of Brutus by complying literally with Brutus' directions while heading for the opposite effect. Thus, he obeys Brutus' order not to blame him (246) by declaring: "if I *were dispos'd* to stir... I *should* do Brutus wrong... I will not do them wrong; I rather choose to wrong the dead, to wrong myself and you..." (III.2.123–128). This is superb nastiness! The only similarity between the two speeches is their general tripartite structure: Introduction – (more or less) rational argumentation – mainly manipulative manoeuvres. In all other respects the two speeches differ totally as the following closer examination will show.

Brutus' speech

Brutus starts with a reference to his "honour", thus trying to establish an authority which does not depend on the conclusiveness of his following statements. In the following sentence he appeals to the rational judgement of his audience. It is this – by no means necessary or convincing – close connection between personal honour and the truth of factual statements or contentions (i.e. that Caesar was ambitious) which paves the way for Antony's famous later attacks on Brutus' honour.

In the second part of his speech Brutus justifies the murder with Caesar's ambition. Brutus offers a simple alternative: Caesar living = you all die as slaves vs. Caesar dead = you all live as free men. He presents no evidence for his assumption that Caesar really was ambitious. This later gives Antony the chance to submit concrete evidence for Caesar's lack of ambition.

In the third part of his speech, Brutus tries to intimidate potential opponents by condemning them as unpatriotic and slave-like underdogs. This, of course, aims at crude rhetorical manipulation of the audience, which flatly contradicts Brutus' former appeal to the wisdom of his audience. On the whole, Brutus' language is stiff, matter-of-fact (prose!), and unemotional: He "informs" ("this is my answer", III.2.21) his audience in a highly stylized way (his speech is full of parallelisms and other rhetorical figures) about the reason for his deed and he expects the audience to accept his justification in the same cool matter-of-fact way. In his speech there are no signs that it was an emotional problem for him to kill his "best lover". Instead, Brutus presents himself as someone who has coolly and objectively compared two values and has decided to accept the higher value, i.e. political freedom instead of personal friendship. Brutus' final evaluation of Caesar reads like a computer outprint: Column 'love': "I weep for him"; column 'courage': "I honour him"; column 'ambition': "I slew him". – end of the program. There are no traces of Brutus' former uncertainty about the reality of Caesar's ambition (cf. in contrast II.1.10–34) or his essential humaneness in his attitude to his wife (cf. II.1.233–303). Although Brutus does not seem to care much for his audience and their expectations, he convinces them for the time being, for they demand: "Let him be Caesar." (52)

Antony's speech

In contrast to Brutus' essentially static speech, Antony's speech is full of dynamics: It starts piano and ends up fortissimo.

Antony opens his speech with a flat lie: "I come to bury Caesar, not to praise him." (III.2.76) The theatre audience, of course, knows too well what Antony is up to (cf. III.1.293–295). This camouflaging of his real intentions by asserting the exact opposite is a pervading characteristic of Antony's whole speech. At first, it may be motivated by understandable caution, but later this "figure of speech" turns more and more into ironical derision of Brutus' orders.

The same is true of Antony's professed appreciation of Brutus' honour and his contention that Caesar was ambitious. In his introduction Antony seems to accept Brutus' claim for honour and his justification of the murder. Only the short interjection "If it were so" (81) signalizes that Antony perhaps considers Caesar's ambition not as a fact but as a more or less questionable hypothesis of Brutus.

In the second part of his speech, Antony fuses Brutus' reference to his honour and his contention of Caesar's ambition into a kind of complex syllogism of the following structure: Brutus is an honourable man – Honourable men are always right – So if Brutus says Caesar was ambitious, it must be true. This is the string of associations Brutus wanted to evoke with the introduction of his speech. Antony now turns this manipulative attempt of Brutus against him by trying to disprove the adequacy of Brutus' accusation against Caesar and thus to destroy Brutus' honour at the same time. This strategy deprives Brutus of the possibility of admitting a faulty judgement without losing his honour and therewith his great public respect. In the end, even the plebeians use the attribute "honourable" with derisive irony: "They were traitors. Honourable men!" (155). Antony ends the argumentative part of his speech with an effective appeal to the emotions of his audience. Like a priest speaking to his community, Antoniy intones, in a very impressive image, his sorrows in order to gain the sympathy of his audience. Rhetorical connoisseurs will appreciate the fact that the pause Antony's heart needs to come out of the coffin again is also an effective means of provoking the desired affirmative reactions from the audience and of thus establishing a vital dialogue with them. Compare Brutus' rather unsophisticated and harsh demand: "If any, speak ... I pause for a reply." (III.2.34/35) to Antony's refined use of rhetorics.

At the end of the second part of his speech, Antony has achieved two important aims: In the eyes of his audience he has seriously questioned Caesar's ambition, and he is also accepted as a most noble man. The worst danger for Antony is over now.

The following parts of Antony's speech rely on mainly manipulative manoeuvres. Alternatively Antony appeals to the material interests (cf. the toying with the contents of Caesar's will) and the emotions of his audience (cf. Caesar's mantle or Brutus' wicked abuse of Caesar's deep love for him). Antony mainly uses two techniques to make his rhetorical appeals more effective:

Indirectness: For instance, Antony does not state his real intentions openly but pretends he means their exact opposite (cf. "I will not do them wrong", III.2.127). He also describes his real intentions or capacities in the conditional (cf. "If I were dispos'd to stir ...", 123; cf. also 218–224). Thus, the audience is informed about possible and, this is the rhetorical implication, in themselves adequate reactions, without having the feeling that someone wants to talk them into certain reactions. Instead, they experience their respective inner reactions as the result of their own volition. A variation of this technique is Antony's toying with Caesar's will. Instead of explaining its contents first, Antony describes in detail the presumptive reactions of his audience and other people if they were to know its contents. Thus, Antony tries to create the desired emotional reaction before its factual cause. When the respective emotions have once been kindled it does not matter any more whether the facts (i.e. Caesar's legacy in this case) really justify such reactions or not.

Extensiveness and exaggeration: For instance, Antony is not satisfied with just stirring his audience, but wants to stir their "hearts *and* minds to mutiny *and* rage" (124; cf. also Antony's invocation of Caesar's blood in 180–196). And concluding from his description of the presumptive reactions to Caesar's will (cf. 134–139), one would expect it to make every Roman a millionaire (cf. in contrast 242–253). Or: Caesar's will will "inflame you, it will make you mad" (146).

By these and other rhetorical means, Antony leads his audience from unconditional acceptance of his person, over the condemnation of the conspirators as traitors and villains, to a climax of destructive and revengeful frenzy, the first victim of which is poor Cinna, the poet.

Antony, the winner, full of – irresponsible – satisfaction, comments on his success: "Now let it work. Mischief, thou are afoot, take thou what course thou wilt." (262–263). In the end, Antony has not succeeded because of better arguments but because of his better rhetoric and his better empathy with his audience. This result supports an understanding of JC as a drama about the workings of politics (where better rhetoric often defeats better arguments) and about two contrasting characters, an ascetic and rationalistic moralist and a sensual and emotional liar. But it is not Antony's "well developed cleverness" which makes him disagreeable, but his lack of responsibility, the horrible consequences of which are displayed in the impressive representation of the rioting mob in III.3.

Verlauf der Stunde

1. Unterrichtsschritt: Brutus' Rede (III.2.13–63)

Die Rede wird zu Beginn von der Kassette vorgespielt. Nachdem ein Schüler seine Zusammenfassung der Rede vorgetragen hat, werden auf der Basis der gemeinsamen Hausaufgabe die Dreigliedrigkeit der Rede (13–17, 18–29, 29–35) und die hauptsächlichen Funktionen der drei Teile (Appell an Rationalität, Begründung und Rechtfertigung der Tat, Diskreditierung möglicher Zweifler) erarbeitet und an der Tafel festgehalten. Bei der anschließenden genaueren Analyse von Brutus' Begründung (18–29) sollten vor allem zwei Punkte herausgearbeitet werden:
– Brutus rechtfertigt sich auch gegenüber dem Vorwurf, einen Freund getötet zu haben – dieser Vorwurf wird später von Antonius erhoben!
– Brutus gibt zwar eine Begründung („ambition"), bleibt aber den Beweis für diesen Vorwurf gegenüber Cäsar schuldig.

Zum Abschluß wird der Gesamteindruck der Rede (knapp, rational, Prosa) ermittelt und zu Brutus' Charakter in Beziehung gesetzt.

2. Unterrichtsschritt: Überblick über Antonius' Rede

Im Unterschied zum Vorgehen bei Brutus' Rede wird die Kassette erst am Ende dieses Schritts vorgespielt.

Zunächst wird auf der Basis der Hausaufgabe der sechsteilige Aufbau der gesamten Rede erarbeitet und an der Tafel festgehalten.

Dieser erste Überblick über die gesamte Rede wird dadurch ergänzt, daß ein Schüler seine Zusammenfassung der Rede vorliest. Bei den folgenden genaueren Analysen der einzelnen Redeteile sollten die Aussagen des Schülervortrags jeweils als vorgegebene Hypothesen im Unterrichtsgespräch diskutiert werden. Bei der gesamten Behandlung dieser Rede sollte die leitmotivische Funktion von „honourable" und die zunehmend ironischere Verwendung dieses Attributs deutlich werden. Berücksichtigt werden sollte schließlich auch der geschickte Wechsel von rationaler Argumentation und emotionalem Appell.

3. Unterrichtsschritt:
Antonius' Gegenbeweise (III.2.75–109)

Bei der Analyse der ersten beiden Teile von Antonius' Rede sollten vor allem die folgenden Punkte herausgearbeitet werden:

– In seiner Einleitung akzeptiert Antonius Brutus' Vorwurf gegen Cäsar als gewichtige, aber zu prüfende Hypothese („if it were so"), die er im zweiten Teil seiner Rede sozusagen diskutiert.
– Im zweiten Teil seiner Rede konfrontiert Antonius die Behauptung der Verschwörer mit seinen eigenen und den Erfahrungen der Zuhörer. Dabei sollte hier als ein wesentlicher Unterschied zu Brutus' Rede der Bezug zu konkreten Dingen als Beweismittel hervorgehoben werden.
– Zum Schluß des ersten Teils seiner Rede appelliert Antonius an die frühere Bewunderung des Volkes für Cäsar.

4. Unterrichtsschritt:
Indirektheit als Mittel zur emotionalen Beeinflussung (III.2.120–162)

Dieser Schritt beginnt mit einer Detailanalyse von 120–129. Zu zeigen ist dabei, daß nicht in dem Gesagten selbst, sondern in dessen Implikationen die rhetorische Raffinesse von Antonius' Vorgehen liegt (vgl. Notes on interpretation).

Anhand der Betrachtung von Antonius' Einführung von Cäsars Testament wird eine Variante des Prinzips der Indirektheit erarbeitet: Antonius teilt den Plebejern zunächst nicht den Inhalt des Testaments mit, sondern beschreibt im Konditional dessen voraussichtliche Wirkung auf die „commoners" und auf seine Zuhörer. Indem er ihnen ihre Reaktionen vorformuliert, erzeugt er genau die gewünschte Reaktion.

5. Unterrichtsschritt:
Antonius' direkter Angriff (III.2.171–211)

Dieser Teil der Rede sollte nicht nur unter inhaltlichen Aspekten, sondern auch im Hinblick auf seine Bühnenwirksamkeit betrachtet werden. Der Rest der Rede (ab 211) wird kursorisch behandelt. Anschließend wird die sich allmählich verändernde Verwendung von „honourable" in Antonius' Rede genauer betrachtet. Zum Abschluß dieses Schritts wird Antonius' Rede, ganz oder in Ausschnitten, von der Kassette vorgespielt.

6. Unterrichtsschritt:
Vergleich der beiden Reden

Zunächst wird Antonius' Rede zusammenfassend charakterisiert und dann Brutus' Rede, auch im Hinblick auf die Wirkung, gegenübergestellt.

7. Unterrichtsschritt:
Konsequenzen

Unter Bezugnahme auf Antonius' selbstzufriedenes Fazit in III.2.262f. werden anhand von III.3. (Cinna, the poet) zunächst die unmittelbaren Konsequenzen der Forumsszene betrachtet. Abschließend werden dann die weiterreichenden Folgen von Brutus' rhetorischer Niederlage für den Gesamtverlauf des Dramas ermittelt.

Hausaufgabe

Die Behandlung des 4. Aktes in der folgenden Stunde hat zwei Schwerpunkte:
- Die Gegenüberstellung der beiden feindlichen Parteien. Der Schwerpunkt liegt dabei auf der „quarrel-scene".
- Die Erscheinung von Cäsars Geist als Vorausdeutung auf den Untergang der Verschwörer.

Zur Vorbereitung dieser Stunde sollten sich die Schüler noch einmal den gesamten 4. Akt vergegenwärtigen und folgende Ausschnitte und die dazugehörigen Fragestellungen gründlich vorbereiten:
1. IV.1.1–35 und IV.3.173–177: Inwiefern wird das bisherige Bild von Antonius bestätigt oder modifiziert, und wie ist die moralische Qualität des Triumvirats einzuschätzen?
2. IV.3.1–28, 63–87, 93–118, 143–151, 200–228: Inwiefern wird unser bisheriges Bild von Brutus und Cassius durch diesen Streit bestätigt bzw. modifiziert?
3. IV.3.248–256, 278–289: Welche dramatische Funktion hat das Erscheinen von Cäsars Geist?

15. Stunde:
Die gegnerischen Parteien

Didaktische Vorbemerkungen

Nachdem im 3. Akt der rhetorische Kampf um das Volk von Antonius gewonnen worden ist, ist die militärische Auseinandersetzung unausweichlich. Bevor im 5. Akt die eigentliche Schlacht beginnt, werden im 4. Akt beide Seiten noch einmal aus „neutraler" Beobachterperspektive gezeigt, wobei das Schwergewicht des Textes und dieser Stunde auf dem spannungsgeladenen Verhältnis zwischen Bru-

tus und Cassius liegt. Das Erscheinen von Cäsars Geist, das auf den bevorstehenden Untergang der Verschwörer vorausweist, wird am Ende der Stunde besprochen.

Bei der Betrachtung der feindlichen Parteien sollten vor allem zwei Punkte herausgearbeitet werden:
- Zum einen der offensichtliche, vor allem moralische Gegensatz zwischen beiden Parteien: Auf der einen Seite wird skrupellos darüber diskutiert, welche Köpfe noch rollen sollen, auf der anderen Seite wird im Rahmen einer gefährdeten privaten Freundschaft um moralische Standards gestritten.
- Zum anderen die Bedeutung der beiden Szenen für unsere Vorstellungen von den Hauptfiguren. Dazu ist es notwendig, die Darstellung der Figuren in diesem Akt mit ihren früheren Darstellungen zu vergleichen.

Notes on interpretation

Before the final battle starts, the audience has the occasion to study both parties separately, and again we are forced to re-evaluate the main figures.

The opening part of IV/1 is an early literary representation of the workings of brains behind the scene. People's lives are reduced to names on a list which are either "pricked", i.e. marked, or not. The language is staccato-like, and even the bargaining about the death of close relatives (cf. 2/3 and 4–6) does not seriously interrupt the efficient proceedings of these managers of the death of about a hundred senators (cf. 177). Almost triumphantly, Antony consents to the death of his nephew: "He shall not live; look, with a spot I damn him" (6). For such people life is a cheap currency, the Roman empire a self-service shop (cf. 13–15), and their own colleague (i.e. Le-

68

pidus) nothing more than a submissive ass.

In the preceeding scenes we got to know many different sides of Antony (as the lover of a gay life, as a skilful dissembler, as an ardent admirer of Caesar, as an emotional, revengeful, and in his revenge irresponsible man, and as a great rhetorician). Although revenge is not a laudable intention as such, it is at least guided by some notion of justice. The Antony we are confronted with at the beginning of act IV is neither interested in revenge, nor in copying Caesar's positive qualities, nor in giving the people their due share of Caesar's legacy, but only in naked power. Thus our last impression of Antony is solely negative. We may have had doubts whether Caesar was really as dangerous as he was depicted by the conspirators, but we are dead certain that Antony and his "friends" should be prevented by all means from coming to power.

Changing from the triumvirate to Brutus and Cassius is like switching from a mafia film to a morality play. While Antony and his party are dividing the Roman empire among themselves, Brutus and Cassius quarrel about moral principles and finally become reconciled to each other as apparently good friends. Nevertheless, a closer examination shows that the quarrel is not motivated by some casual misunderstanding, but by the great contrast between the two characters, which we have noted several times before: Brutus, the idealist, still insists on moral aims and means (cf. IV.3.18–28) – and therefore chides Cassius for protecting corruptibility. Cassius, on the other hand, cannot understand Brutus' nagging criticism of "every nice offence" (IV.3.7/8) in their present fatal situation.

Brutus' idealism, though, is not without flaws because Brutus again tries to shut his eyes before reality and its essential un-cleanliness and inconsequence. He chides Cassius for not sending him the necessary money to pay his soldiers and explains his reproach with the memorable explanation: "For I can raise no money by vile means" (71). Apparently, Brutus expects Cassius to do the dirty work for him so that his own "honesty" can remain without a flaw. This kind of moral inconsequence (which here almost verges on hypocrisy) is not accidental but a central feature of Brutus' half-hearted involvement in the conspiracy which comes best to the fore in his absurd lament "O that we then could come by Caesar's spirit, and not dismember Caesar!" (II.1.169/170). Considering this background, Cassius' indignation becomes more understandable and Brutus' Caesar-like self-righteousness (Cf.: "For I am arm'd so strong in honesty", 77; cf. Caesar's "But I am constant as the northern star", III.1.60) more unpalatable.

The untimely quarrrel between Brutus and Cassius is another symptom of the generally desperate situation of the conspirators. They can hope for no support from outside, neither from the people of Rome, nor from the peasants around Philippi who "stand but in a forc'd affection" (207). Under these circumstances, Brutus' hopeful statements "our cause is ripe" (217) and "We ... are ready to decline" (219) are full of tragic irony. The appearance of Caesar's ghost to Brutus clearly signalizes that "fate" is working against the conspirators. Lines 248–256 show that Brutus feels anxious, unsettled, and lonely, and therefore orders his guards under some spurious pretext to sleep in his tent. In this context, the question is of minor importance whether the ghost is meant to be a – subjective – hallucination of Brutus (cf. "Macbeth" where only Macbeth sees Banquo's ghost) or an – objective – supernatural phenomenon (cf. "Hamlet", where the ghost of Hamlet's father is seen by several people). In both cases, the appearance of Caesar's ghost is a bad omen, signifying either that Brutus has lost all faith in the success of his cause (and will therefore fail) or that the objective circumstances (supernatural spheres included) are so unfavourable that defeat is unavoidable. We will discuss this question of human freedom more thoroughly in the following lesson.

Verlauf der Stunde

1. Unterrichtsschritt:
Antonius' Skrupellosigkeit (IV.1.1–35, IV.3.173–177)

Zu Beginn der Stunde trägt ein Schüler die Ergebnisse seiner Hausaufgabe vor, die im folgenden Unterrichtsgespräch ergänzt bzw. korrigiert werden. Folgende drei Punkte, die die Skrupellosigkeit von Antonius und seinen Triumviratskollegen zeigen, sollten herausgearbeitet werden:
– Antonius' geplanter Betrug am Volk: Er will einen Teil von Cäsars Hinterlassenschaft an das Volk für eigene Zwecke abzweigen (vgl.IV.1.8/9).
– Antonius' menschenverachtende Einstellung zu Lepidus (vgl. IV.1.12–40)
– Die Geschwindigkeit, mit der über den Tod selbst engster Verwandter (vgl. Lepidus' Bruder) beschlossen wird, und die große Anzahl der geplanten Morde (vgl. IV.3.173–177).

Anschließend wird im Unterrichtsgespräch die Bedeutung dieser Szene für unser Bild von Antonius erarbeitet. Es sollte deutlich werden, daß hier eine neue und ausgesprochen negative Seite von Antonius zum Ausdruck kommt. Es folgt eine Zusammenstellung aller wesentlichen Charakteristika von Antonius (vgl. TA).

2. Unterrichtsschritt:
Die „quarrel-scene" (IV.3.1–28, 63–87, 93–118, 143–151, 200–228)

Die Behandlung des Streits zwischen Brutus und Cassius bildet den Schwerpunkt dieser Stunde. Zunächst gibt ein Schüler einen Überblick über den Verlauf des Streits. Anschließend werden im Unterrichtsgespräch als faktische Basis des Streits Brutus' drei Vorwürfe gegenüber Cassius (Deckung von Bestechungen, eigene Bestechlichkeit, Verweigerung von Soldgeldern) geklärt und deren Berechtigung erörtert. Dabei sollte auf Cassius' schon bekannte Skrupellosigkeit hingewiesen werden. Offenbar ahnt Brutus hier zum ersten Mal, daß Cassius keineswegs so nobel ist, wie er bisher gedacht hatte. Anhand einer genauen Analyse der Verse 18–28 und 65–77 wird dann Brutus' Idealismus als Hauptursache für seine Erregung herausgearbeitet und vor dem Hintergrund von Cassius' kritischer Einlassung (7/8) diskutiert.
Zu Anfang sollte der Lehrer darauf hinweisen, daß es sich bei Vers 23 („for supporting robbers") um einen Flüchtigkeitsfehler des Dramatikers handelt (bisher war Cäsar von Brutus immer nur „ambition" vorgeworfen worden). Bei der Diskussion sollten auch die folgenden Punkte berücksichtigt werden:
– Brutus' an Cäsar erinnernde Arroganz (vgl. 67)
– Ähnlich wie beim Attentat will sich Brutus auch bei der Soldbeschaffung möglichst nicht die Finger schmutzig machen. Aus dieser Perspektive erscheint Cassius' Empörung mehr als verständlich.

Die wichtigsten Ergebnisse der Diskussion werden an der Tafel in Form einer Gegenüberstellung von Brutus und Cassius festgehalten.

Zum Abschluß dieses Unterrichtsschritts werden der Streit und die abschließende Versöhnung unter dem Beziehungsaspekt betrachtet: Wie war die bisherige Entwicklung der Beziehung der beiden Figuren, und wie hat sie sich durch den Streit verändert? Es sollte deutlich werden, daß nach der Versöhnung Cassius wieder in die Rolle des Befehlsempfängers zurückfällt. Der Verlauf der Beziehung wird an der Tafel in einem einfachen Diagramm festgehalten.

3. Unterrichtsschritt:
Cäsars Geist (IV.3.248–256, 278–289)

Zum Abschluß dieser Stunde wird auf die melancholische Stimmungslage von Brutus (vgl. 248–256) und die Bedeutung der Erscheinung von Cäsars Geist eingegangen. Dabei sollte auch kurz die Frage der „Realität" des Geistes diskutiert werden. Der Lehrer kann die Ambiguität von Geistern in Shakespeares Dramen anhand von „Hamlet" (mehrere Personen sehen den Geist von Hamlets Vater, vgl. I.1) und „Macbeth" (nur Macbeth sieht den Geist von Banquo, vgl. III.4) verdeutlichen.

Hausaufgabe

In der folgenden Stunde wird mit dem Untergang der Verschwörer die sukzessive Behandlung des Dramas abgeschlossen. Dabei steht im Mittelpunkt die Frage, warum die Verschwörer untergehen. Die Schüler sollen zu Hause den 5. Akt kursorisch lesen und ausgewählte Passagen V.1.72–119, V.3.23–96, V.5) unter der genannten Fragestellung genauer betrachten. Darüber hinaus sollen sie sich frühere und jetzige Fehlentscheidungen von Brutus zusammenstellen.

16. Stunde:
Das Ende der Verschwörer

Didaktische Vorbemerkungen

Spätestens nach dem vierten Akt ist klar, daß der Untergang der Verschwörer besiegelt ist. Leitfrage bei der Behandlung des 5. Aktes in dieser Stunde ist daher, *warum* die Verschwörer die Schlacht verlieren. Der Text bietet die folgenden drei Erklärungen an:
1. Militärische und andere Fehlentscheidungen
2. Vorzeitige Resignation
3. Walten des Schicksals.

Zu Beginn der Stunde wird die Frage geprüft, inwiefern falsche militärische und andere Entscheidungen zu dem Untergang der Verschwörer geführt haben. In den beiden folgenden Unterrichtsschritten werden dann die beiden anderen konkurrierenden Erklärungen genauer untersucht.
Die Stunde schließt mit einem kurzen Resümee von Brutus' „Karriere". Damit ist die sukzessive Behandlung des Dramas abgeschlossen. Die in dieser Stunde nur im Hinblick auf den 5. Akt besprochene Schicksalsproblematik wird in der 17. Stunde zusammenfassend für das gesamte Drama behandelt.

Notes on interpretation

In act V, Antony's revenge is finally brought about with the death of the two leading conspirators. Order is restored and Antony can be magnaminous and acknowledge Brutus' essential honour which he had so ironically questioned in his forum speech.

The drama on the whole allows different explanations of the conspirators' final failure.

On the level of action the failure is obviously the result of fatal former decisions and actions of Brutus, to which are added two military mistakes (wrong strategy, premature attack) in the last act.

On a deeper level of interpretation, Brutus' mistakes can be understood as consequences of serious flaws in his character. All of Brutus' mistakes have in common that they relate to the world of action and that the respective decisions were made against Cassius' explicit advice. Thus, Brutus' moral deficiency does not only consist of his unrealistic idealism but also of his failure to realize his incompetence in practical matters. On the contrary, he rather arrogantly claims that he is a soldier at least of equal standing with Cassius (cf. IV.3.31–35, 205–227). Brutus' arrogance and lack of self-knowledge contribute heavily to his failure.

Premature resignation is another important factor in question: On their last meeting, the two friends are almost obsessed with their future defeat: Cassius the practical rationalist and Epicurean, suddenly takes notice of bad omens, and Brutus, when confronted with possible public shame, draws back from his professed stoicism. Apparently, both conspirators lack confidence and have lost their philosophical orientation. Cassius' makes a rather pointless reference to his birthday (V.1.72), considering the actual situation, implying that it might be the day of his death as well. This association is more explicitly repeated by Cassius in V.3.23–25, before he has even received the bad (and wrong) news (30–32) from Pindarus. Instead of demanding a more thorough inspection Cassius calls Pindarus back ("come down; behold no more", 33) and kills himself. Cassius' precipitation is stressed twice by Titinius (cf. 65 + 84). Obviously, Cassius has resigned before the battle is really lost (cf. Titinius: "... did not they put on my brows this wreath of victory...", 81/82) and perhaps has lost it for this very reason.

Although Brutus does not immediately despair after Cassius' suicide (cf.: "We shall try fortune in a second fight", V.3.110), he soon gives in: "Slaying is the word; it is a deed in fashion" (V.5.4/5).

To be sure, after Brutus' many mistakes, the conspirators have little reason for excessive optimism. On the other hand, there are no conclusive reasons for the deep resignation they display. So we are inclined to conclude that their morale has broken down under the stress of the final battle. This – rather flat – psychological explanation ignores the roles which fate and Caesar's spirit play in this drama.

In his only monologue (III.1.255–274) Antony lays a curse on the conspirators and prophesies that "Caesar's spirit, ranging for revenge" (271) will come over them. And Antony's curse comes true, not only with respect to its final intention (revenge) but also literally: Caesar's ghost appears twice to Brutus (cf. V.5.17–19), and both conspirators refer to Caesar before their suicide (cf. V.3.41/42; 45/46; V.5.50/51). In addition, both conspirators feel that they are under the influence of some adverse fate. Seen from this point of view, the resignation of Brutus and Cassius would not be the consequence of a weak psyche but of the impact of superhuman powers or mechanisms.

When fate or chance are involved in a drama we have to ask whether it is "blind" fate or "pure" chance or whether these powers are used by the dramatist as agents of poetic justice. To answer this question is the task of an overall interpretation of the drama.

Verlauf der Stunde

1. Unterrichtsschritt:
Brutus' Fehlentscheidungen

Ein Schüler trägt die Ergebnisse seiner Hausaufgaben vor, die an der Tafel festgehalten und ggf. im Unterrichtsgespräch ergänzt werden (vgl. Tafelanschrieb). Anschließend wird nach den Gemeinsamkeiten dieser Fehlentscheidungen gefragt: Sie betreffen fast alle praktische Fragen und werden meist von Brutus gegen den besseren Rat von Cassius durchgesetzt. Während die früheren Fehler auf Brutus' schon besprochenen realitätsfremden Idealismus zurückzuführen sind, zeigen die letzten beiden Fehler, daß Brutus seine eigenen praktischen Fähigkeiten überschätzt und Cassius in dieser Hinsicht unterschätzt. Dieses Faktum wird verdeutlicht durch Rückgriff auf drei kurze, bisher noch nicht besprochene Ausschnitte aus der „quarrel scene" (IV.3.30–34, 51–60, 200–205). Damit ergibt sich, neben Brutus' Idealismus, seine falsche Selbsteinschätzung als weitere Ursache für das Scheitern der Verschwörung.

2. Unterrichtsschritt:
Resignation oder Schicksal? (I)

Im Mittelpunkt dieses und des folgenden Schritts stehen die zu Hause vorbereiteten zentralen Szenen des 5. Aktes, in denen die fatale Mischung von Resignation und Schicksalsglaube der beiden Verschwörer deutlich zum Ausdruck kommt.
Begonnen wird mit Cassius' „Monolog" (Messala ist dabei nur Statist) in V.1.72–92. Bereits hier sollte das Problem der fatalen Korrespondenz zwischen Resignation und Schicksalsgläubigkeit andiskutiert werden: Resigniert Cassius, weil er neuerdings an Schicksalsvorausdeutungen glaubt, oder zieht er diese heran, weil

er innerlich resigniert hat? Anschließend wird der Abschied der beiden Freunde (93–119) betrachtet. Dabei sollte auch die dramatische Funktion dieser Szene als Vorausdeutung auf das Ende berücksichtigt werden.

3. Unterrichtsschritt:
Resignation oder Schicksal? (II)

In diesem Schritt werden die beiden Selbstmorde behandelt. Bei Cassius' Selbstmord sollte deutlich werden, daß er nur oberflächlich Folge eines tragischen Irrtums, tatsächlich aber die Folge vorzeitiger (?) Resignation (aufgrund böser Vorzeichen?) ist. Die entscheidenden Textpassagen (V.3.20–46, 63–71, 80–96) werden im Unterricht gelesen.
Anschließend wird Brutus' Selbstmord (V.5.16–51) behandelt, der zu einem Zeitpunkt stattfindet, zu dem die Schlacht tatsächlich verloren ist. Hier kommt es vor allem auf zwei Punkte an, nämlich auf Brutus' offensichtlichen Glauben an das Fortwirken von Cäsars Geist (V.5.17–19, 50 f.; diese Passagen werden oft herangezogen, um den Titel des Dramas zu rechtfertigen) und auf seine trotz allem positive Bilanz seines Lebens (34–38).

4. Unterrichtsschritt:
Epilog

Die sukzessive Behandlung von JC schließt mit einer kurzen Betrachtung von Antonius' Epilog auf Brutus (V.5.68–75), der zeigt, daß Brutus' „honesty" selbst von seinem schärfsten Gegner anerkannt wird. Eigene (V.5.34–38) und fremde (V.5.68–75) Lebensbilanz stimmen also im Falle von Brutus überein.

Hausaufgabe

In der folgenden Stunde werden die Vorzeichen und ihre Funktionen zusammenfassend behandelt. Zur Vorbereitung der Stunde sollen die Schüler folgende, z. T. schon früher behandelte Passagen im Hinblick auf Vorzeichen und deren Funktionen zu Hause in zwei Gruppen analysieren:
1. Gruppe: I.2.1–25, I.3.1–78
2. Gruppe: II.2.1–90, III.1.1–12

17. Stunde:
Vorausdeutungen und das Problem der menschlichen Freiheit

Didaktische Vorbemerkungen

Schlechte Vorzeichen, die sich alle bewahrheiten, bestimmen JC wie kaum ein anderes Drama von Shakespeare. Jeder der beiden Hauptteile der Handlung (Cäsars Ermordung und der Untergang der Verschwörer) wird von einem bösen Vorzeichen (Warnung vor den Iden des März bzw. Antonius' Fluch) dominiert. Die Menschen scheinen in einer von Göttern und Schicksalsmächten weitgehend vorherbestimmten Welt zu leben, die kaum noch Raum für menschliche Willensfreiheit und Verantwortung läßt.

Diesen Merkmalen eines Schicksalsdramas stehen andere Passagen gegenüber, in denen Vorzeichen entweder als Aberglauben in Frage gestellt oder von Skeptikern (z. B. Cassius oder Decius) nach eigenem Belieben manipulativ uminterpretiert werden. Von einer Schicksalstragödie unterscheidet sich JC schließlich auch dadurch, daß die Figuren, zumindest Cäsar, ihrem Unheil hätten ausweichen können.

Ausgehend von Formen des Aberglaubens in der Gegenwart werden zunächst allgemeine Charakteristika von Vorzeichen und die generelle Ambivalenz der Vorzeichen in JC erarbeitet und am Beispiel der Iden des März genauer untersucht. Als dramatische Funktionen der Vorzeichen lassen sich die Erzeugung von Spannung und die Profilierung von Cäsars Hybris als seiner Schuld herausarbeiten. Im vierten Schritt werden die die Verschwörer betreffenden Vorzeichen als Mittel auktorialer Kritik an der Verschwörung bestimmt. Abschließend werden die Ergebnisse an der Tafel zusammengefaßt und diskutiert.

Notes on interpretation

"Superstition" is a label for a group of rather diverse phenomena like magic, curses, astrology, different forms of fortune-telling and different kinds of omens etc. It is mainly used to separate right – Christian – faith from false pagan or pseudo-religious beliefs and practices, although the borderline is not so easy to define. Many of us consider ourselves to be good Christians, but are afraid of black cats crossing the street in front of us or have horoscopes worked out for us before serious decisions. Often, we have a playful attitude to superstition; in some circles it is chic to be a little superstitious.

Most forms of superstition, especially omens and fortune-telling, are the expression of our fears of the future, which we try to manipulate by the observance of certain rules ("Never do . . .!"). By getting to know the future in advance we try to prevent exactly that which was predicted – which is really contradictory and therefore absurd.

Omens and fortune-telling, taken seriously, really presuppose the total determination of our lives. As this is an intolerable idea to man, omens or oracles are often formulated as obscure riddles (cf. the Delphic oracle). Their meanings are not clear (cf. the thunderstorm in JC) or they are formulated as warnings in order to evade the negative event.

The action of JC is dominated by two omens, the warnings of the ides of March to Caesar, and Antony's curse of the conspirators. In the following we shall examine what the characters think about omens and to what degree they have freedom of action.

In JC omens and other forms of superstition are much disputed. The only person who fully believes in omens is Casca to whom they represent messages from the gods. His warning "let not men say 'These are their reasons – they are natural'" (I.3.29/30) shows that probably also in Shakespeare's times many people tried to explain strange phenomena rationally. But even Casca is not really sure about the exact meaning of the thunderstorm and the strange phenomena accompanying it ("strife in heaven" or punishment for the "too saucy" world, cf. I.3.11–13). Except at the end of the drama, Cassius does not believe in omens, he even defies them (cf. I.3.43–52) and explains to Brutus: "The fault, dear Brutus, is not in our stars, but in ourselves..." (I.2.141/142). Cicero formulates a "sceptical theory" of omens: "But men may construe things after their fashion, clean from the purposes of the things themselves" (I.3.34/35). There are two notable examples in the drama which can be understood as providing evidence for Cicero's thesis. In both cases, omens are re-interpreted in a way that suits the purposes of the interpreter: Cassius re-interprets the thunderstorm in order to win Casca for the conspiracy (I.3.53–79), Decius re-interprets Calphurnia's dreams in order to prevent Cae-

sar from staying at home (II.2.83–90; cf. also II.1.202–211). In both cases, people's superstition makes them easy victims of manipulation.

Caesar himself wavers. Cassius says of him that he has "grown superstitious of late" (II.1.195). On his first appearance in the drama we see him urging Antony to follow the fertility ceremony exactly, later on he drives the soothsayer away as a troublesome dreamer (I.2.25). In II.2, Caesar twice changes his position. First, he dismisses the omens, then he yields to Calphurnia's entreaties only to change his opinion again when Decius offers him a more positive interpretation of Calphurnia's dreams. From Caesar's former harsh treatment of Calphurnia (cf. in contrast Brutus-Portia) we may conclude that his yielding is less the result of his love for his wife than the indication of his inner uncertainty about the validity of the omens.

The omens concerning the ides of March are mainly of the warning type, that is, Caesar could have survived if he had stayed at home – if you happen to believe in omens! The course of the action is apt to support superstition, for events follow Calphurnia's dreams almost literally (several wounds, people bathing their hands in Caesar's blood). So we are to take the respective omens seriously and have to ask why Caesar did not.

There are two critical situations in II.2 where Caesar decides against the omens, and both display severe faults in his character, namely megalomania (41–48) and susceptibility to flattery (91). Thus, Caesar's faults are the real cause of his death, not some doubtful predetermination. He is guilty and is punished for it. This result is valid, whether we believe in omens or whether we take them as literary devices to make that point. Caesar had freedom of action and misused it with respect to the norms of the drama.

The problem is more difficult in the case of Antony's curse of the conspirators. A curse is, by its intention, a prediction which leaves no alternative to the person affected by it – supposing that the curse really exerts its magic function, which it seemingly does in our case: Caesar's ghost appears twice to Brutus, Cassius suddenly changes his opinion on omens, and both conspirators die in the end. In addition, they display a remarkable lack of confidence all through act V.

Although JC is full of omens and predictions which "really work", it is not a tragedy of fate where the figures have no freedom of action. Caesar obviously decided arrogantly against the godly warnings, and Brutus freely decided to join the conspiracy and made his wrong decisions even against Cassius' advice. If Brutus was a victim, he was the victim of Cassius' persuasion but not of any supernatural powers. After Antony's curse, though, his destruction seems to be predetermined by the author's "poetic justice".

There is one notable exception, though, in the drama which cannot be interpreted in this way, and that is Cinna, the poet: In his dream he received a clear warning to leave the house. Athough he wants to obey the omen, he leaves the house under some strange compulsion ("yet something leads me forth", III.3.4) and is killed by the rioting plebeians. Cinna is clearly an innocent victim of evil forces.

Verlauf der Stunde

1. Unterrichtsschritt: Hinführung

Zu Beginn der Stunde wird über Formen und Ausmaß von Aberglauben in der Gegenwart diskutiert. Auf diese Weise sollen die Schüler erfahren, daß diese The-

matik keineswegs antiquiert ist. Vor allem sollen sie sich auch mit den philosophischen bzw. religiösen Voraussetzungen von Aberglauben beschäftigen. Im einzelnen sollten folgende Punkte angesprochen werden:

– Gründe für Aberglauben: z.B. Angst vor der Zukunft; Versuch, die Zukunft zu manipulieren
– Philosophische Implikationen: mehr oder weniger starke Determiniertheit der Zukunft durch das Schicksal bzw. göttliche Mächte; dementsprechende Einschränkungen der menschlichen Willensfreiheit und Schuldfähigkeit
– Die Begriffsbildung „Aberglauben" als Mittel zur Abgrenzung der Mehrheit gegenüber einer Minderheit.

2. Unterrichtsschritt: Vorzeichen und ihre Problematisierung

Anhand von I.3.1–78 wird die ambivalente Darstellung von Vorzeichen in JC erarbeitet. Dem „gläubigen" Casca werden die Skeptiker Cicero und Cassius gegenübergestellt. An Cascas Dialogbeiträgen wird zweierlei deutlich:

– Vorzeichen werden als Warnungen der Götter betrachtet (I.3.12–13 und 53–56).
– Ganz ähnlich wie heute gab es offenbar auch schon zu Shakespeares Zeiten den Versuch, scheinbar übernatürliche Phänome als natürliche zu erklären (vgl. I.3.28–32).

Die skeptische Position wird in dieser Szene in Form von „These" (Cicero, I.3.33–36) und „Beweis" vertreten (vgl. Cassius' „Uminterpretation" von Cascas Deutung für seine eigenen Zwecke in den Versen 83–90; ähnlich verfährt Decius mit der Deutung von Calphurnias Träumen in II.2.83–90). Im Endeffekt bleibt offen, auf wen oder was sich die Vorausdeutung bezieht: auf alle, auf Cäsar, oder auf das Schicksal der Verschwörung. Wichtig in diesem Zusammenhang ist auch Cassius' Bemerkung „The fault, dear Brutus, is not in our stars, but in ourselves" (I.2.140–142).

3. Unterrichtsschritt:
Die Iden des März

Die im vorausgehenden Unterrichtsschritt erarbeitete ambivalente Bewertung von Vorzeichen in JC erlaubt es nun, die kumulierten Vorzeichen vor Cäsars Ermordung als dramatisches Mittel zur Darstellung von Cäsars fataler Hybris (und damit seiner Schuld) und zur Erzeugung von Spannung zu verstehen.

Zunächst werden kurz alle im Zusammenhang mit Cäsars Ermordung auftretenden Vorzeichen an der Tafel gesammelt und als den Betroffenen nicht völlig determinierende warnende Vorausdeutungen bestimmt: Cäsar hätte durchaus überleben können, wenn er die Vorzeichen als göttliche Warnungen akzeptiert hätte.

Anschließend wird Cäsars – ambivalente – Einstellung zu Vorzeichen und sein Umgang mit ihnen genauer betrachtet. Leitfrage ist hier, warum Cäsar trotz böser Omen doch zum Capitol geht. Dafür sollten die folgenden drei Erklärungen angeführt werden:
– Schicksalsergebenheit oder Stoizismus (II.2.26–37)
– Hybris (38–48); diese Erklärung kann durch frühere Ergebnisse über Cäsars Charakter gestützt werden
– Anfälligkeit für Schmeichelei (vgl. II.1.202–208; II.2.83–91 und 105–107).

Die Vorzeichen werden damit als Mittel zur Darstellung von Cäsars Schuld bestimmbar. Dabei ist es gleichgültig, ob man an Vorzeichen glaubt oder nicht.

Zum Abschluß dieses Schritts werden die möglichen dramatischen Funktionen der Vorzeichen in Bezug auf den Leser/Zuschauer diskutiert. Dabei sind unterschiedliche Funktionszuweisungen möglich, je nachdem, ob der Zuschauer selbst an Vorzeichen glaubt oder nicht: Im ersten Fall haben sie für ihn den Charakter von Vorausdeutungen. Trotzdem wird er darauf gespannt sein, ob Cäsar die göttlichen Warnungen befolgt oder nicht. Im zweiten Fall erlebt der Zuschauer die zusätzliche Spannung, ob sich die Warnungen im Verlauf des Dramas bewahrheiten oder nicht.

4. Unterrichtsschritt:
Antonius' Fluch

Die die Verschwörer betreffenden Vorzeichen sind schon in der vorhergehenden Stunde behandelt worden. Hier werden sie als Konsequenzen von Antonius' Fluch in III.1.255–274 bestimmt. Anschließend wird die Frage erörtert, welche dramatische Funktion der Fluch hat. Zum Abschluß wird herausgearbeitet, daß den beiden sukzessiven Haupthandlungssträngen (Cäsars Ermordung, Untergang der Verschwörer) zwei Vorzeichenkomplexe (Iden des März, Antonius' Fluch) entsprechen.

5. Unterrichtsschritt:
Zusammenfassung der erarbeiteten Ergebnisse

Zum Abschluß der Stunde werden die dramatischen Funktionen der Vorzeichen in JC an der Tafel (vgl. Tafelanschrieb) zusammengefaßt und die Frage der Willensfreiheit in JC diskutiert.

Hausaufgabe

In der abschließenden Stunde sollen drei verschiedene Ansätze zur Gesamtdeutung des Dramas in Form einer „debate" diskutiert werden. Die Stunde wird durch eine arbeitsteilige Hausaufgabe vorbereitet: Jede Gruppe soll sich auf die Verteidigung einer der folgenden Thesen vorbereiten und Argumente gegen die jeweils anderen beiden Thesen sammeln:
1. JC is a political tragedy.
2. JC is the tragedy of idealism.
3. JC is a drama of character.

18. Stunde:
Ansätze zu einer Gesamtdeutung von JC

Didaktische Vorbemerkungen

In der abschließenden Stunde sollen unterschiedliche Ansätze zu einer Gesamtdeutung des Dramas diskutiert werden. Ziel ist es dabei nicht, eine „richtige" Interpretationsperspektive zu finden; die Schüler sollen vielmehr erkennen, daß unterschiedliche Fragestellungen oder Interessen zu unterschiedlichen Sichtweisen des Dramas führen.
Die Stunde verläuft in Form einer „debate": Es werden sukzessive drei zu Hause arbeitssteilig vorbereitete Deutungsthesen vorgetragen und kritisch diskutiert. Ein Schüler trägt zunächst die erste These vor und begründet sie möglichst schlüssig. In der folgenden Debatte verteidigt die entsprechende Schülergruppe die These, während die anderen Schüler versuchen, die ganze These oder Teile von ihr zu erschüttern. Entsprechend wird bei den anderen beiden Thesen verfahren. Da damit der Unterrichtsverlauf weitgehend de-

Zusatztext zur 18. Stunde

Generally, the Brutus-image falls into one of four patterns:
1. Brutus as the Republican who fails because he lacks practical understanding of men and politics;
2. Brutus as the moral idealist who induces disorder in his own soul and in the Roman state by committing himself to violence on insufficient evidence but on the highest abstract principles;
3. Brutus as the "noblest Roman" who is trapped by Cassius and lesser men into a fatal choice which he finally repents;
4. Brutus as the essentially unappealing, cold, egocentric leader who, in his refusal to heed the counsels of others, comes close to a kind of Caesarism.

Aus: Hartsock, Mildred E.: The Complexity of JC. *PMLA* 81 (1966), S. 57.

finiert ist, enthält der Anhang für diese Stunde kein Stundenblatt, sondern nur einen Tafelanschrieb.
Die Thesen selbst (vgl. „Verlauf der Stunde") sind absichtlich überspitzt formuliert, damit eine möglichst lebhafte Diskussion in Gang kommt. Die wichtigsten Pro- und Contra-Argumente werden an der Tafel festgehalten. Allerdings werden dabei die „didaktischen" Überspitzungen der Thesen und deren Plausibilität nicht dokumentiert. Da der Tafelanschrieb sehr ausführlich ist, haben wir in dieser Stunde auf „Notes on interpretation" verzichtet.
Die in dieser Stunde berücksichtigten Interpretationsperspektiven sind keineswegs erschöpfend. Werden für die abschließende Besprechung des Dramas zwei Stunden verwendet, können noch fol-

gende interessante zusätzliche Probleme behandelt werden:
- „private" (character, friendship) vs. „public" (roles, ideas or ambitions)
- Die Frage der ästhetischen Qualität des Dramas und die damit zusammenhängende Frage des Dramentitels
- Brutus als vieldeutiger Held des Dramas. Vgl. dazu den Zusatztext von M. E. Hartsock.

Verlauf der Stunde

1. Unterrichtsschritt:
JC als politisches Drama

These: JC ist vor allem ein politisches Drama. Im Mittelpunkt steht das tragische Scheitern einer Verschwörung zur Verteidigung der Demokratie vor einem blutigen Tyrannen.

JC ist sicher auch ein politisches Drama, aber nicht in erster Linie. Deutlich werden sollte hier, daß unsere Demokratievorstellungen auf das elisabethanische Zeitalter und die Dramenwelt von JC nicht übertragbar sind.

2. Unterrichtsschritt:
JC als Idealismuskritik

These: Im Mittelpunkt des Dramas steht die Kritik von weltfremdem und daher gefährlichem Idealismus, verkörpert durch Brutus.

Die Schüler sollten hier vor allem verstehen, daß zwar der Gegensatz von Idealismus und Realismus ein zentrales Thema des Dramas ist, daß aber die besondere Tragik des Stücks gerade darin besteht, daß der moralische Idealismus zu schwach ist, um sich gegen unmoralischen Realismus durchzusetzen. Im Grunde werden beide Seiten durch das Drama kritisiert,

wenn auch wegen unterschiedlicher Defekte.

3. Unterrichtsschritt:
JC als Charakterdrama

These: Im Mittelpunkt von JC steht die Komplexität des menschlichen Charakters, die an den Hauptfiguren verdeutlicht wird.

Diese These faßt einen wichtigen Aspekt des Dramas, ist aber in dieser Formulierung zu einseitig, weil sie diesen einen Aspekt auf Kosten der anderen zuvor behandelten Aspekte verabsolutiert. An diesem Beispiel sollte zum Abschluß deutlich werden, daß man gerade ein Drama wie JC nicht auf eine Bedeutung oder einen Dramentypus festlegen sollte: JC ist weder ein politisches Drama noch ein Ideendrama noch eine Charaktertragödie, sondern eine Mischung von allen drei Dramentypen. Es kommt daher nicht von ungefähr, daß JC des öfteren Shakespeares „problem plays" zugerechnet wird.

Tafelanschrieb:

<u>Global perspective on JC</u>

<u>JC as a political tragedy</u>

<u>pro</u>	<u>contra</u>
political story	mainly depiction of characters and their private problems
Brutus' political idealism	totally unpolitical plebeians
Caesar's megalomania	Caesar is at most a potential tyrant
important political morale: revolutions lead to chaos	general atmosphere of fatalism

<u>JC as a criticism of idealism</u>

the conspiracy fails because of Brutus' idealism	the failure of Brutus' idealism is fatal to Rome's future; Brutus' idealism serves to criticize brutal realists like Cassius or Antony
the realists, Antony and Octavius, are the winners	the realist Cassius dies, too

<u>JC as an analysis of human complexity</u>

the moral quality of all main characters is ambiguous	Antony is clearly a villain; all conspirators (except Brutus) are simply selfish
different aspects of the main characters are shown (private side, public role, attitude to death etc.)	the characters are not complex but contradictory (= serious defect of JC)
	the depiction of human complexity is only one aspect of the drama

10. Stunde: Brutus' Entscheidung		Julius Caesar

Unterrichtsschritte	Unterrichtsformen Fragestellungen / Impulse, Arbeitsaufträge	Erwartungen / Ergebnisse
1. Unterrichtsschritt: Brutus' Selbstrechtfertigung Text: II. 1. 10–34	Kassette / Unterrichtsgespräch – Place this monologue within the context of the play. – What is Brutus' central problem in this monologue? – Explain Brutus' personal attitude to Caesar. – How does Brutus judge Caesar's previous political actions and decisions? – What is Brutus afraid of? – What reasons does Brutus give for his fears? – Brutus is having, as it were, an argument with himself. Comment on the predominant characteristics of his language in this passage. – Comment on lines 28–34: What do they tell us about Brutus' trust in his own argument? What are the characteristics of his language here?	In I. 2. Cassius tried to win Brutus for a conspiracy against Caesar. Brutus promised to think about it. It is now up to him to come to a decision. It is rather obvious that without Brutus' participation there will be no conspiracy. To be able to reconcile the idea of Caesar as he has known him up to now and his fears of Caesar's future development: "How that [being crowned] might change his nature". He loves him as a friend and has no reason to criticize him. Brutus has no reason to criticize him. Caesar never let his decisions be unduly influenced by emotions. He fears that after being crowned Caesar may change and turn into a tyrant. Brutus has no substantial evidence for his fears; he can only refer to commonly held ideas ("common proof") about the behaviour of ambitious people. 1. Not argumentative but metaphorical. Threetimes Brutus compares Caesar to dangerous animals (adder, kind of wasp, serpent). Apparently, he wants to convince himself of Caesar's dangerous nature. 2. The extensive use of the conditional (may, might, would) shows his uncertainty. Apparently, Brutus does not think much of his own argument: He invents again a negative hypothesis about Caesar's future development. Its obvious that Brutus is yet not sure about his decision and tries to justify his intention to join the conspiracy.
2. Unterrichtsschritt: Brutus' Entscheidung Text: II. 1. 44–58	Unterrichtsgespräch – What happens in this short scene? – How does Brutus react?	Brutus gets letters which urge him to do something. He understands the letters as hints at his brave ancestors and feels flattered. He wants to measure up to his ancestors and promises to take action, believing that will substantially improve the present conditions.

© Ernst Klett Verlage GmbH u. Co. KG, Stuttgart 1988. Alle Rechte vorbehalten.

Unterrichtsschritte	Unterrichtsformen Fragestellungen / Impulse, Arbeitsaufträge	Erwartungen / Ergebnisse
3. Unterrichtsschritt: Brutus' Alpträume Text: II. 1. 61–69 und 77–85	Kassette / arbeitsteiliger Arbeitsauftrag 1. What does this monologue tell us about Brutus' state of mind after his decision? 2. Explain the central images and their function.	I. 61–69: 1. Brutus has been in a state of great inner agitation (no sleep), he feels split and unreal. 2. Brutus tries to express his inner state of mind by using three comparisons: He compares his emotional state to a phantasma or hideous dream and his mental state first to council of opposing parties, then to a state of civil war. The images show his inner conflict. II. 77–85: 1. Brutus realizes that he is embarking on a horrible adventure which only can be successful when accompanied by furtiveness. 2. In order to express his emotional aversion to a conspiracy, he compares it to a most detestable monster, which can only survive by masking itself.
4. Unterrichtsschritt: Zusammenfassung der erarbeiteten Ergebnisse	Unterrichtsgespräch	**Tafelanschrieb:** Brutus' Monologues (II. 1.)

Monologue	Contents and function
II. 1. 10–34	Brutus tries to find a justification for the murder. Result: What Caesar <u>may</u> develop into. Shows his inner uncertainty.
II. 1. 44–58	Brutus feels confirmed and flattered by (Cassius') anonymous letters. Final decision on the murder, <u>if</u> redress will follow.
II. 1. 61–69	Expresses Brutus' inner agony about the conspiracy by means of comparisons ("hideous dream", "insurrection").
II. 1. 77–85	Reflects again Brutus' inner aversion but shows that he accepts the necessity of disguise.	
Hausaufgabe:	Read II. 1. 86–190 carefully and analyze the passage with respect to the following questions: 1. What is the function of Brutus' first address to his fellow conspirators? 2. Why is Brutus against the assassination of Antony? Are his arguments reasonable? Consider also the final consequences of Brutus' decision!	

© Ernst Klett Verlag GmbH u. Co. KG, Stuttgart 1988. Alle Rechte vorbehalten.

1. Stunde: Shakespeares Werk / Hinführung zu „Julius Caesar"		Julius Caesar

Unterrichtsschritte	Unterrichtsformen Fragestellungen / Impulse, Arbeitsaufträge	Erwartungen / Ergebnisse
1. Unterrichtsschritt: Shakespeares Werk Arbeitsgrundlage: Worksheet No. 1 (Famous Quotations)	Unterrichtsgespräch – The following list consists of famous quotations. Find in each case the adequate proverbial translation. Where do these quotations come frome? – The sources of the quotations are written on the blackboard in three columns. Find adequate headlines for them.	Cf. Worksheet No. 1 auf Stundenblatt S. 2 Comedies, Histories, Tragedies
2. Unterrichtsschritt: Shakespeares Biographie Arbeitsgrundlage: Zusatztext zur 1. Stunde	Schülerreferat Unterrichtsgespräch – Shakespeare has been dead for almost 400 years. What difficulties are therefore to be expected when reading a Shakespeare drama?	**Tafelanschrieb:** Shakespeare's Life Born: 1564 (baptized April 26) in Stratford-on-Avon Schooling: local grammar school Family: married Anne Hathaway in 1582, three children Profession: playwright and actor in London, very successful Later Years: lived as a country gentleman in Stratford Death: 1616 (his will was made in March 1616) Different world picture, different historical situation, different language.
3. Unterrichtsschritt: Der historische Cäsar Arbeitsgrundlage: Worksheet No. 3 (History of Rome)	Unterrichtsgespräch / Lehrervortrag – What do you know about Caesar? – Look at the map on the Worksheet. Which modern countries belonged to the Roman Empire in Caesar's time?	Portugal, Spain, France, Belgium, Holland, parts of Germany, Italy, the Yugoslav coast, Albania, Bulgaria, Greece, Turkey, Syria, the Lebanon, Israel, southern Mediterranean coast, Tunisia.
4. Unterrichtsschritt / Hausaufgabe:	Arbeitsauftrag (bis zum Beginn der 5. Stunde) – Read the drama carefully. Write a short summary of each of the five acts and find an adequate headline for each act. The summary should describe the function of the individual act as regards the total action of the play. – Analyze the function(s) of the first scene.	

© Ernst Klett Verlage GmbH u. Co. KG, Stuttgart 1988. Alle Rechte vorbehalten.

Hausaufgabe:	Teil 1) für alle Schüler (Arbeitsgrundlage: Worksheet No. 1 zur 2. Stunde): Read the text on the Worksheet carefully and note down all the deviations from modern English. Try to categorize your findings. Teil 2) arbeitsteilig für 4 Gruppen (Arbeitsgrundlage: Worksheet No. 2 zur 2. Stunde): (groups A – C): Find all the deviations from modern English and try to categorize them. (group D): Explain the images in example 9 and 10. Hierbei sollten bei Passagen aus JC die zugrundegelegte englische Ausgabe und bei Verständnisschwierigkeiten die Übersetzung zu Rate gezogen werden. Bei der Herstellung der Schülerkopien des Worksheet No. 2 rechte Spalte abdecken!

Worksheet No. 1

Famous Quotations

1. To be, or not to be, that is the question
2. For Brutus is an honourable man
3. It was the nightingale and not the lark
4. Something is wrotten in the state of Denmark
5. Let me have men about me that are fat
6. Have you prayed to-night, Desdemona?
7. Though this be madness, yet there's method in't
8. Why, I will see you at Philippi, then
9. There are more things in heaven and earth, Horatio, than are dreamt of in your philosophy
10. But soft! methinks, I scent the morning air
11. The tooth of time
12. The time is out of joint
13. That is the true beginning of our end
14. Much ado [= 'Lärm'] about nothing
15. The rest is silence
16. Thy wish was father, Harry, to that thought
17. Love's labour's lost
18. A horse! A horse! My kingdom for a horse!

1. Sein oder Nichtsein, das ist hier die Frage (Hamlet III, 1)
2. Denn Brutus ist ein ehrenwerter Mann (JC III, 2)
3. Es war die Nachtigall und nicht die Lerche (Romeo and Juliet II, 2)
4. Etwas ist faul im Staate Dänemark (Hamlet I, 5)
5. Laßt dicke Männer um mich sein (JC I, 2)
6. Hast du zur Nacht gebetet, Desdemona? (Othello V, 2)
7. Der Wahnsinn hat Methode (Hamlet II, 2)
8. Bei Philippi sehen wir uns wieder (JC IV, 3)
9. Es gibt mehr Dinge zwischen Himmel und Erde als eure Schulweisheit sich träumen läßt (Hamlet I, 5)
10. Mir deucht, ich wittre Morgenluft (Hamlet I, 5)
11. Der Zahn der Zeit (Measure for Measure, V, 1)
12. Die Zeit ist aus den Fugen (Hamlet I, 5)
13. Das ist der Anfang vom Ende (Midsummer Night's Dream V, 1)
14. Viel Lärm um nichts
15. Der Rest ist Schweigen (Hamlet V, 2)
16. Der Wunsch war der Vater des Gedankens (Henry IV, IV, 4)
17. Verlorene Liebesmüh
18. Ein Pferd! Ein Pferd! Ein Königreich für ein Pferd! (Richard III, V, 4)

© Ernst Klett Verlage GmbH u. Co. KG, Stuttgart 1988. Alle Rechte vorbehalten.

2. Stunde: Elisabethanisches Englisch

Unterrichtsschritte	Unterrichtsformen Fragestellungen / Impulse, Arbeitsaufträge	Erwartungen / Ergebnisse
1. Unterrichtsschritt: Sprache eines elisabethanischen Sachtextes Arbeitsgrundlage: Worksheet No. 1 (The True Reportory of the Wracke)	Unterrichtsgespräch – What deviations from modern English usage did you find in the text on Worksheet No. 1? – Let us find some linguistic categories in order to classify the deviations in the text.	Cf. Handout Cf. Handout
2. Unterrichtsschritt: Sprachproben aus Shakespeare's Dramen Arbeitsgrundlage: Worksheet No. 2 (Characteristics of Elizabethan English)	Unterrichtsgespräch – What deviations from modern English usage did you notice in the passages from Shakespearian dramas on Worksheet No. 2? – Now let us categorize our results again.	Cf. Handout Cf. Handout
3. Unterrichtsschritt: Bildersprache Arbeitsgrundlage: Worksheet No. 2	Vortrag der Hausaufgabe	Cf. Handout
4. Unterrichtsschritt: Funktion von Vers und Prosa Arbeitsgrundlage: Worksheet No. 2	Lektüre / Analyse / Lehrervortrag – What is the main difference between example No. 2 and No. 4 on the Worksheet? – Analyze the dominant metre of these verses. What are its main characteristics? – Who used blank verses in German literature?	No. 2 is written in verse, No. 4 in prose Five iambic feet, no rhymes = 'blank verse' E. g.: Goethe, Lessing, Schiller, Kleist, Hebbel, Hauptmann

© Ernst Klett Verlage GmbH u. Co. KG, Stuttgart 1988. Alle Rechte vorbehalten.

Unterrichtsschritte	Unterrichtsformen Fragestellungen / Impulse, Arbeitsaufträge	Erwartungen / Ergebnisse
1. Unterrichtsschritt: Das Image des elisabethani-schen Theaters Arbeitsgrundlage: Worksheet No. 1 (Map of London) Arbeitsgrundlage: Worksheet No. 2 (A German Traveller Reports)	Unterrichtsgespräch – Look at the map of London on the Work-sheet. How many theatres can you find? Where are they located and what other buildings are in the neighbourhood? – What conclusions can be drawn from the map about the social role of the theatres? Take into account that London had about 200.000 inhabitants at that time and that a theatre could hold up to 3000 spectators. – What do we learn from the text "A German Traveller Reports" about theatrical perform-ances in Elizabethan times?	Six resp. seven (with the later "Hope"): On the South Bank: The Swan, The Hope, Globe Theatre, Rose Theatre. On the North Bank: The Curtain, The Fortune, The Blackfriars. Location: Outside the City limits (exception: The Blackfriars, a private theatre). Neighbourhood: Bear baiting, arena, prison, hospitals. Conclusions: a) part of mass entertainment (cf. bear baiting), b) bad reputation (banned from the city like prisons and hospitals), c) great popularity (room for about 10% of the population) Theatre performances were very popular ('almost every day', 'very numerous audiences', 'excessive applause'); the atmosphere was that of mass entertain-ment (dances, music, smoking, drinking, eating), cf. TA.
2. Unterrichtsschritt (fakultativ): Argumente der Theater-gegner Arbeitsgrundlage: Worksheet No. 3 (A Letter to the Archbishop)	Unterrichtsgespräch – Which are the Lord Mayor's main argu-ments against the theatres? [Kernsatz auf Folie] – What does the fact that the Lord Mayor asks the Archbishop for help suggest about the relationship between Church and State?	– Corruption of the youth – Religion is neglected – Work is neglected – Immoral audience – Cover-up for criminal activities Both institutions have similar interests and work closely together.
3. Unterrichtsschritt: Das Publikum des elisabe-thanischen Theaters Arbeitsgrundlage: Worksheet No. 4 (The Globe Audience)	Unterrichtsgespräch – Characterize the typical audience of the Globe Theatre. Of which two groups did they mainly consist? – What difficulties arise for the dramatist from such an audience? How can he best solve these problems?	a) People without seats: the so-called "groundlings" stood on the ground and consisted of shopkeepers, craftsmen, lower bourgoisie, apprentices and young people. b) People with seats: in the gallery sat gentlemen of various degree, professional men, courtiers and members of the nobility. Higher members of the nobility were seated at the side of the stage or in "shilling rooms". He is confronted with a variety of tastes and interests. The "groundlings" were mainly interested in entertainment, whereas the more educated people also expected subtle thought and psychology. The dramatist, therefore, had to combine "soap opera" and crude effects with serious drama in his play. He had to rely on rather general topics which were interesting for all members of his audience, cf. TA.

© Ernst Klett Verlage GmbH u. Co. KG, Stuttgart 1988. Alle Rechte vorbehalten.

Unterrichtsschritte	Unterrichtsformen Fragestellungen / Impulse, Arbeitsaufträge	Erwartungen / Ergebnisse
4. Unterrichtsschritt: Vergleich: elisabethanisches und heutiges Theater	Unterrichtsgespräch (anhand des TA) – Now, let's compare the Elizabethan theatre with our modern theatre. What is its reputation (location, audience . . .) like?	Cf. TA
5. Unterrichtsschritt: Die elisabethanische „apron stage" Arbeitsgrundlage: Worksheet No. 5 und 6 (Shakespeare's Theatre; The Atmosphere in an Elizabethan Theatre)	Schülerreferat	Cf. TA
6. Unterrichtsschritt: Dramaturgische Gegebenheiten von „apron stage" und „Guckkastenbühne" („fourth-wall stage")	Unterrichtsgespräch – Imagine a modern realistic theatre performance. What might happen at the beginning? – Compare this beginning with that in an Elizabethan theatre. What would have happened there? – Where would you rather be an actor – in an Elizabethan or in a modern theatre? Give reasons. – Compare the two kinds of theatre with respect to what they demand of the audience.	The light might be turned out, the curtain raised and we look into an often glaringly illuminated, realistically furnished room. Some people might be sitting in armchairs, talking. No curtain, the stage is almost empty, lit by daylight. Maybe, one or two actors walk through the doors at the backside onto the stage and start talking. In an Elizabethan theatre: closer contact to the audience, I can see their reactions, they can see my miming; I don't need to shout as much. In the Elizabethan theatre, much more imagination is demanded of the spectators because of its restricted scenery and the lack of artificial lighting. In modern theatre, on the other hand, the illusion is frequently interrupted by changes of scenery.

© Ernst Klett Verlage GmbH u. Co. KG, Stuttgart 1988. Alle Rechte vorbehalten.

Tafelanschrieb:

	Elizabethan Theatre	Modern Theatre
Location	outside the city limits, close to prison, hospitals, places for mass entertainment	fully integrated into the city centre
Reputation and function	bad reputation, but very popular as mass entertainment (drinking, eating etc.); cf. modern football stadiums	good reputation, but not too popular (subsidies necessary!); refined form of elite entertainment
Official evaluation	strong condemnation by Church and State because of immorality, subversiveness, and coarseness	fully accepted as important part of cultural life, occasional scandals on moral or political grounds
Audience	very heterogeneous; mainly two groups: "groundlings" (lower bourgeoisie) and the higher ranks on the galleries (nobility, business and professional men)	rather homogeneous, mainly educated middle-class ("Bildungsbürgertum")
	different tastes and interests → very general topics, mixture of different levels etc.	difficulty to reach the less educated → informal theatre in streets, old factories etc.
Problems for the author → solution		
Form of stage – consequences	"apron stage" (ca. 14 × 9 m), protruding far into the audience (ca. 18 × 18 m) → intimacy between actors and audience → great subtlety of voice, gesture and expression	"fourth-wall stage" ("Guckkastenbühne") → distance → less subtlety
Ligthing	only daylight → same light for actors and spectators (they can see each other!) → intimacy	artificial light (many effects possible) → actors can't see spectators → distance
Curtain	no curtain → continuity of performance → no break in the illusion	curtain → lack of continuity, several interruptions → breaks in the illusion
Scenery	only individual things like a gate, a tree the scenery has to be evoked by → language → no limit to the number of scenes → quick change of location possible	very elaborate and realistic scenery possible
Costumes	lavish and imposing	depending on the style of performance
Demands on spectators	much imagination	less imagination

© Ernst Klett Verlage GmbH u. Co. KG, Stuttgart 1988. Alle Rechte vorbehalten.

Beilage zu 925142, **Seite 7**

© Ernst Klett Verlage GmbH u. Co. KG, Stuttgart 1988. Alle Rechte vorbehalten.

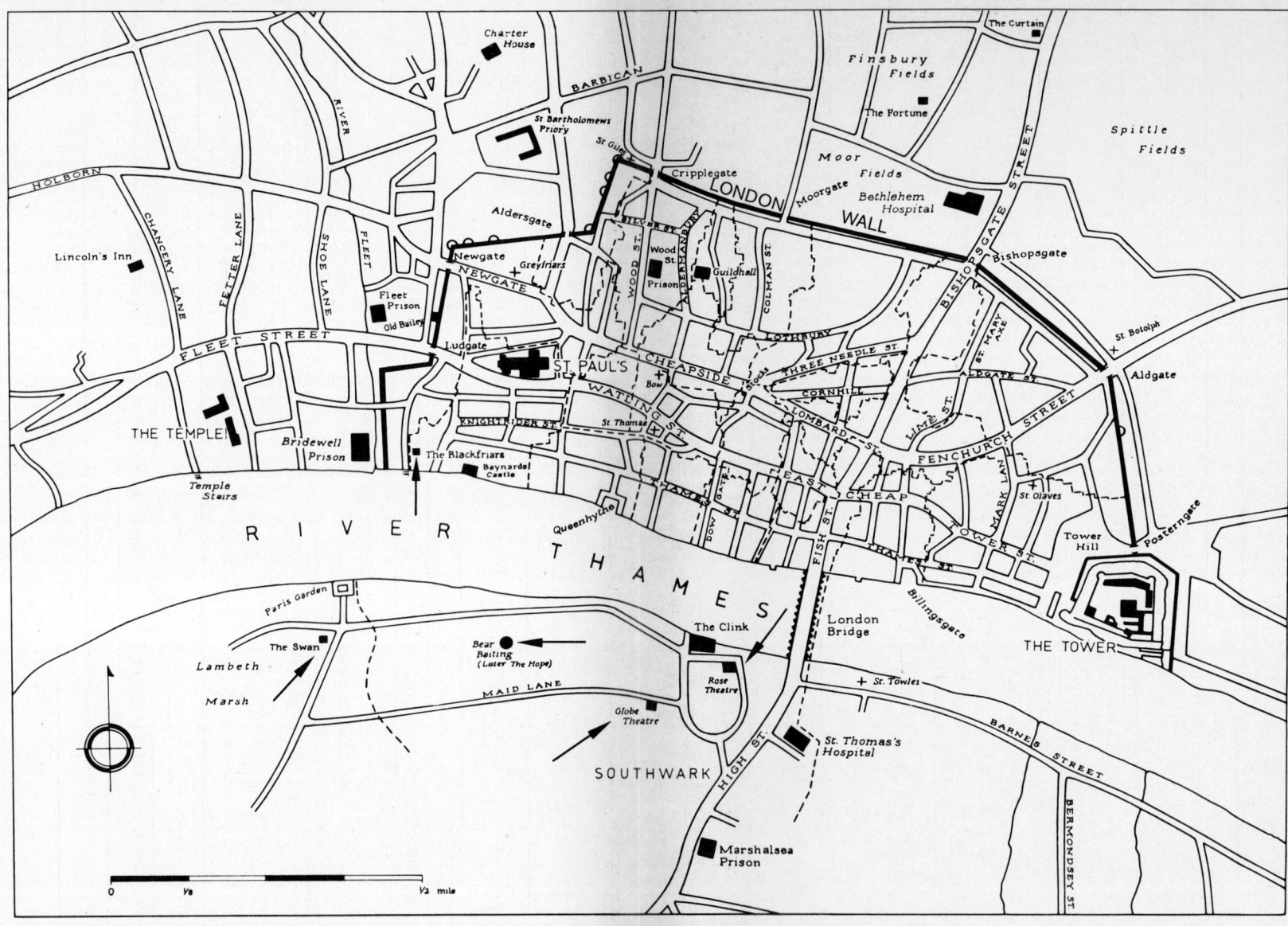

→ = Theatres

Map of London in Shakespeare's time

Aus: *Life-Language-Literature*. Stuttgart: Ernst Klett Verlag 1982, S. 221

Unterrichtsschritte	Unterrichtsformen Fragestellungen / Impulse, Arbeitsaufträge	Erwartungen / Ergebnisse
1. Unterrichtsschritt: Erarbeitung einer Handlungs- übersicht	**Unterrichtsgespräch** – What is the central story of the drama? – What headings for the individual acts, relating them to the central story, have you found?	The history of a conspiracy against Caesar. Cf. TA
2. Unterrichtsschritt: Detaillierung der Handlungs- übersicht	**Unterrichtsgespräch** – Which are the most important events for the conspirators and their fate? – Try to represent the conspirators' fate in the form of a simple line. Show the general positive and negative developments. **Arbeitsauftrag** – Mark the main events (those mentioned before and additional ones) with dots on that line. Place them with respect to the different acts. – Construct a similar line for Caesar's party and mark the main events on it.	Brutus' decision to join the conspiracy, Caesar's assassination, the Forum speeches, war with the triumvirate, Cassius' and Brutus' suicide Cf. TA Cf. TA Cf. TA

© Ernst Klett Verlag GmbH u. Co. KG, Stuttgart 1988. Alle Rechte vorbehalten.

Unterrichtsschritte	Unterrichtsformen Fragestellungen / Impulse, Arbeitsaufträge	Erwartungen / Ergebnisse
3. Unterrichtsschritt: Analyse des Handlungs-verlaufs	Unterrichtsgespräch – Explain the importance of the drama's main events with respect to the general development of the action. – Give a formal description of the drama's action by using terms like "rising" or resp. "falling" action and "turning point". Refer to both parties. – Comment on the title of the drama, bearing in mind the total development of the action. Diskussion – Has the drama a good or a bad ending?	Any summary of the drama's contents which connects the events marked in the TA in a reasonable way. Cf. also "Notes on interpretation". In the first two acts, the action is "rising" for both parties: Caesar is approaching the crown, his opponents are getting organized at the same time. Although the conspirators achieve their aim, Caesar's assassination, this is only a temporary turning point of the action. The real turning is the sweeping effect of Antony's funeral oration. From then onwards, the fates of the two parties develop in opposite directions: For the conspirators, it is a falling for Caesar's followers a rising action. Caesar, the title figure, dies in the third act, though his ghost still influences other characters' actions. The drama's focal character is really Brutus, his ideals and scruples. The drama's ending is ambiguous and its evaluation depends therefore on the reader's interpretation of the drama.
Hausaufgabe:	– Read l. 2. 38–178 carefully and try to answer the following two questions: 1. What means does Cassius use in order to persuade Brutus to support a plot against Caesar? 2. What do we learn about the characters of Cassius and Brutus from this passage?	

© Ernst Klett Verlage GmbH u. Co. KG, Stuttgart 1988. Alle Rechte vorbehalten.

Tafelanschrieb:

The action of JC

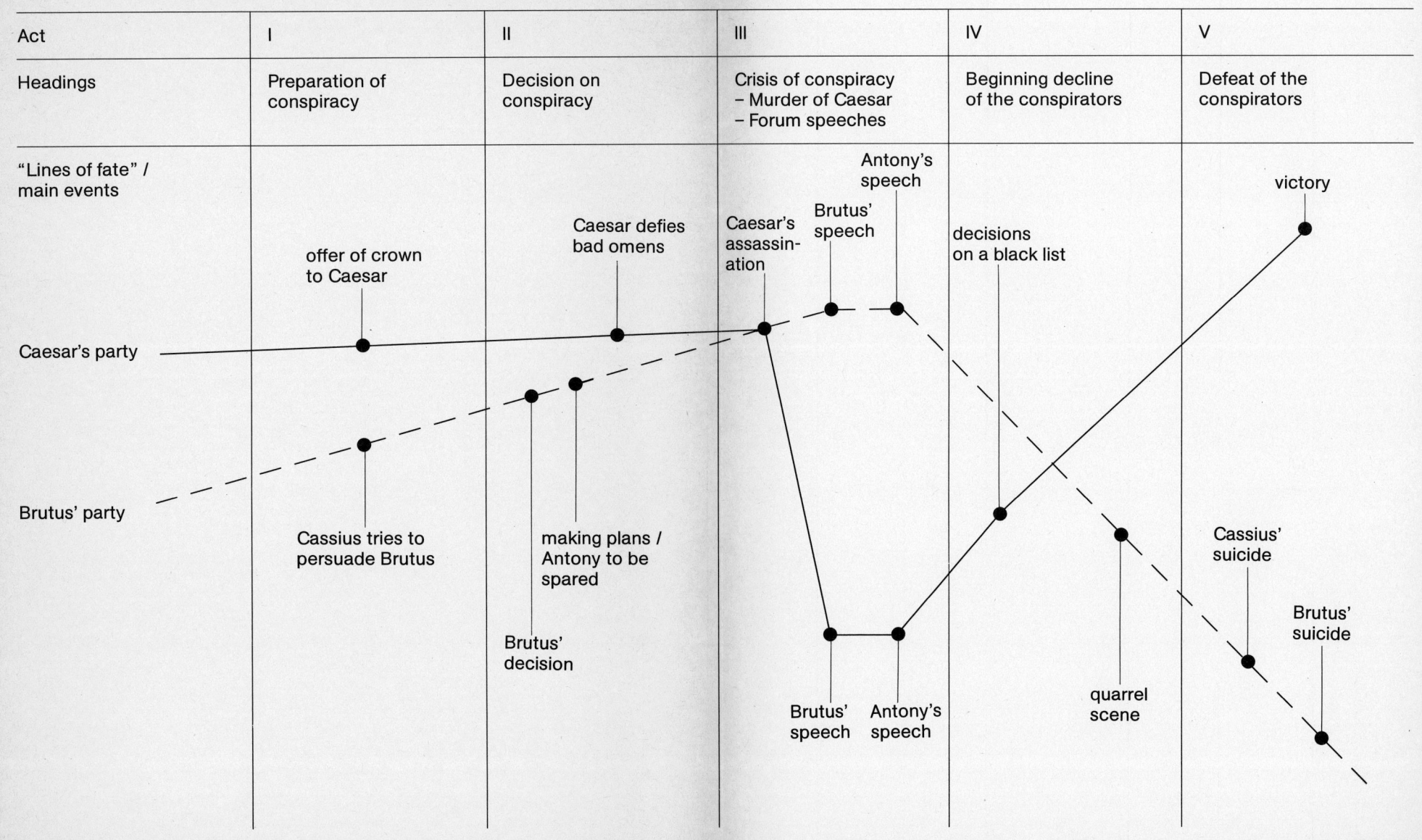

Act	I	II	III	IV	V
Headings	Preparation of conspiracy	Decision on conspiracy	Crisis of conspiracy – Murder of Caesar – Forum speeches	Beginning decline of the conspirators	Defeat of the conspirators

"Lines of fate" / main events

Antony's speech

Brutus' speech

victory

Caesar defies bad omens

Caesar's assassin-ation

decisions on a black list

offer of crown to Caesar

Caesar's party

Brutus' party

Cassius tries to persuade Brutus

making plans / Antony to be spared

Brutus' decision

Brutus' speech   Antony's speech

quarrel scene

Cassius' suicide

Brutus' suicide

© Ernst Klett Verlag GmbH u. Co. KG, Stuttgart 1988. Alle Rechte vorbehalten.

Unterrichtsschritte	Unterrichtsformen Fragestellungen / Impulse, Arbeitsaufträge	Erwartungen / Ergebnisse
1. Unterrichtsschritt: Bedeutung der Textstelle Text: I. 2. 33–178	Unterrichtsgespräch – What has happened before Brutus and Cassius meet for the first time? – Which are the two main functions of this dialogue?	Introduction of Caesar, the title figure, indirectly in I. 1, directly at the beginning of I. 2 during some kind of ceremony. 1. Introduction of two central characters 2. Actual beginning of the action
2. Unterrichtsschritt: Analyse von I. 2. 33–90	Arbeitsauftrag – Which are Cassius' two aims in this dialogue? – Analyze and explain Cassius' communicative strategy and Brutus' reactions to it in this part of the dialogue.	Cf. TA Cf. TA
3. Unterrichtsschritt: Analyse von I. 2. 91–162	Arbeitsauftrag – Analyze and explain Cassius' communicative strategy in this part of the dialogue. Which are his two central arguments against Caesar's godlike position in Rome? – By what means does Cassius try to stir Brutus emotionally?	Cf. TA Cf. TA
4. Unterrichtsschritt: Analyse von I. 2. 163–178	Unterrichtsgespräch – Cassius' rhetoric – a success or a failure? Pay attention to Brutus' former, present and further reactions.	Although Brutus promises in this passage only to think about Cassius' arguments, his reactions indirectly show that he shares Cassius' misgivings with respect to Caesar's godlike position: Cf. TA. Brutus' reactions in earlier parts of this dialogue also show that he seriously considers some action against Caesar.
Hausaufgabe:	Analyze the following passages with respect to the way in which (means, contents) they contribute to our picture of Caesar: Group 1: I. 1. 31–33, 70–77; I. 2. 1–25; II. 2. 1–56 Group 2: I. 2. 80–163; II. 1. 10–27; II. 2. 57–128 Group 3: I. 2. 236–275; I. 3. 72–89; III. 1. 32–77.	

© Ernst Klett Verlage GmbH u. Co. KG, Stuttgart 1988. Alle Rechte vorbehalten.

Tafelanschrieb:

Rhetorics of persuasion I

(Brutus – Cassius I. 2)

A) Cassius' aims

- to find out about Brutus' attitude to Caesar ("testing")
- to win Brutus for a conspiracy against Caesar ("persuasion")

B) Cassius' strategies

accent on "testing"

appeal to friendship / reproach (33–37)

pretence (mirror image): Cassius offers to help Brutus understand himself better (52–59, 67–71)

flattery (58, 63, 91)

self-praise (51, 73–79)

citation of neutral 'witnesses' (59–63)

accent on "persuasion"

reference to honour and self-esteem (93–97)

rational arguments:
Caesar's dominant position is intolerable because
- Caesar is not better than we are (98–100, 143–151)
- Caesar is physically weak (two examples: 101–119, 120–132)
- it defies Roman history (154–158)

emotional arguments:
- It is our own fault: we behave like underlings (140–143)
- reference to Brutus' famous ancestor: indirect flattery and admonition (160–162)

Brutus' reactions

defense: inner struggle (38–48)

Brutus is on his guard (64–66); he disapproves of Caesar being chosen as king (80); he asks Cassius to come to the point (84/85); he stresses his concern for honour and the general good (86–90)

Cf. "results" below

C) Results (163–176)

Brutus gives no clear answer to Cassius' indirect request to do something against Caesar:
- no decision but
- ready to discuss the subject again
- acknowledges the importance of the problem
- concedes the likeliness of an intolerable situation

© Ernst Klett Verlage GmbH u. Co. KG, Stuttgart 1988. Alle Rechte vorbehalten.

7./8. Stunde:
„Charakter" Cäsars

Unterrichtsschritte	Unterrichtsformen Fragestellungen / Impulse, Arbeitsaufträge	Erwartungen / Ergebnisse
1. Unterrichtsschritt: Charakterisierungsmittel	Unterrichtsgespräch – What means of characterization do you know?	Cf. TA
2. Unterrichtsschritt: Einführung Cäsars Text: I. 1. 31–33, 70–77	Arbeitsauftrag / Unterrichtsgespräch – What do we learn generally about Caesar from this passage? – Compare the opinions of the two groups (citizens and tribunes) about Caesar. – Explain the function of this indirect introduction of Caesar.	Caesar is very powerful and has just come back from a victorious battle. Opposite evaluations: The people admire and cheer him, the tribunes disapprove of his growing superiority. It creates curiosity about Caesar.
3. Unterrichtsschritt: Cäsars erster Auftritt Text: I. 2. 1–25	Kassette / Unterrichtsgespräch – Explain the setting of this short scene. – Comment on Caesar's treatment of Calphurnia. – Is Caesar superstitious? – What do we learn about Caesar's position in this scene?	Some kind of public religious ceremony (the Lupercal celebrations). It is very rude to show Calphurnia up in public because of her sterility. The answer is contradictory: He apparently believes in the Lupercal rite but ignores the – important – warning of the soothsayer. Caesar is the unquestioned boss who gives orders which are followed submissively by his underlings.

© Ernst Klett Verlag GmbH u. Co. KG, Stuttgart 1988. Alle Rechte vorbehalten.

Unterrichtsschritte	Unterrichtsformen Fragestellungen / Impulse, Arbeitsaufträge	Erwartungen / Ergebnisse
4. Unterrichtsschritt: Perspektive der Verschwörer Text: I. 2. 80–163	Gruppenvortrag (Basis: Hausaufgabe) / Unterrichtsgespräch Comment on Brutus' attitude to Caesar.	Brutus loves Caesar as a private person but is worried about his superiority as a public figure.
I. 2. 236–275	– Explain Cassius' attitude to Caesar in I. 2. 91–163. – What do we learn from Casca's report about Caesar?	Cassius thinks that Caesar's superior position is unjustified and that it violates Roman tradition. In addition, Cassius is envious and hates Caesar personally. 1. If we agree with Casca's view, Caesar only refused the crown for tactical reasons. He really would have gladly accepted it. 2. The people admire Caesar all the more for refusing the crown. 3. Caesar has a serious physical infirmity, i. e. epilepsy.
I. 3. 72–89	– Explain Cassius' interpretation of the apocalyptic thunderstorm. Comment also on the language he uses.	Cassius wants Casca to understand the thunderstorm as a heavenly warning to Caesar and compares the effect of Caesar with that of a thunderstorm and other cosmic disturbances.
II. 1. 10–27	– Explain Brutus' view of Caesar in these lines.	Brutus has no cause to criticize Caesar who has always kept the balance between reason and emotions. But Brutus is afraid Caesar might develop badly (i. e. become a tyrant) in future.
5. Unterrichtsschritt: Cäsar privat Text: II. 2	Arbeitsauftrag – Explain the dramatic function of this scene.	The conspiracy has already been sealed and exactly planned. In this scene, Calphurnia's warnings offer Caesar a last chance.
II. 2. 1–56	– How does Caesar react to Calphurnia's bad dreams and her interpretation of them?	1. He orders the priests to perform sacrifices at once. 2. He twice arrogantly points out his superiority over all threats. 3. He explains to Calphurnia that the time of death is in the hands of the gods, therefore man cannot do anything to escape it = stoic position. 4. In the end he gives way to Calphurnia's intense begging and decides to stay at home.
II. 2. 57–107	– Explain Decius' rhetorical strategy and its effect on Caesar.	Decius gives a positive and for Caesar flattering explanation of Calphurnia's dreams and "informs" Caesar that the Senate has decided to offer him the crown. Caesar cannot resist this flattery and decides to go to the Senate in spite of all warnings.
II. 2. 108–128	– What do we learn about Caesar from his treatment of the conspirators?	Caesar is very relaxed, kind and considerate.

© Ernst Klett Verlag GmbH u. Co. KG, Stuttgart 1988. Alle Rechte vorbehalten.

Unterrichtsschritte	Unterrichtsformen Fragestellungen / Impulse, Arbeitsaufträge	Erwartungen / Ergebnisse
6. Unterrichtsschritt: Cäsars „imperial style" Text: III. 1. 32–77	Kassette / Unterrichtsgespräch – How does Caesar react to the petitions on behalf of Publius Cimber? Consider especially his language. – Comment on Caesar's last words. What do they show?	Caesar never doubts his own decisions and wouldn't admit to be susceptible to flattery. He arrogantly compares himself with cosmic elements like the northern star or Olympus. Caesar's last words show how much he esteemed and relied on friendship in general and especially on that of Brutus.
III. 1. 255–258	– What is Antony's final judgment on Caesar?	Antony deplores the death of "the most noble man that ever lived".
7. Unterrichtsschritt: Zusammenfassung	Unterrichtsgespräch – Try to give a summary of Caesar's character.	Cf. TA

Hausaufgabe:	1. What do we learn about Brutus (= group 1) and Cassius (= group 2) from the following passages: I. 2. 29–178, 191–215, 309–323; I. 3. 53–130, 157–160; II. 1. 35–58? Describe their attitudes towards friends, Caesar, Rome, and other values. How are they judged by other people? 2. What do we learn about Brutus from II. 1. 234–303 (Brutus – Portia)? Compare this passage with II. 2. 8 – 56 (Caesar – Calphurnia).

© Ernst Klett Verlage GmbH u. Co. KG, Stuttgart 1988. Alle Rechte vorbehalten.

Tafelanschrieb:

Means of characterization

1. Self-explanation
2. Deeds (verbal + physical)
3. Judgements and reactions by other figures

Caesar

	Positive qualities	Negative qualities
Others	successful warrior (the people) modest: refuses crown (the people) loved by Brutus "the noblest man that ever lived" (Antony) not unduly influenced by emotions (Brutus)	very dangerous because forever craving more power = (potential) tyrant (tribunes, Cassius, Casca, Brutus) physically weak, nothing special (Cassius)
Caesar	Self-explanations: valiant no fear whatsoever above flattery constant and just in his decisions superhuman (northern star, Olympus) Deeds: successful warrior kind and considerate deep friendship with Brutus	physical defects: deaf ear, epilepsy, sterile (?) rude to Calphurnia bossy indecisive superstitious (?) susceptible to flattery arrogant, self-conceited

Ambivalences

Positive
successful warrior
true friendship
guided by reason

↕

Negative
ambitious, tyrant (?)
proud and self-conceited
indecisive
physical defects

Private man
physical defects
indecisive
sometimes nice
true friendship (Antony, Brutus)

↕

Public man
powerful, successful warrior
proud and self-conceited
ambitious / potential tyrant (?)

© Ernst Klett Verlage GmbH u. Co. KG, Stuttgart 1988. Alle Rechte vorbehalten.

Unterrichtsschritte	Unterrichtsformen Fragestellungen / Impulse, Arbeitsaufträge	Erwartungen / Ergebnisse
1. Unterrichtsschritt: Vergleich der Hausaufgaben Text: I. 2. 29–178; 191–215 I. 2. 309–323 I. 3. 53–130, 157–160 II. 1. 35–58, 234–303 II. 2. 8–56	Gruppenarbeit (Basis: Hausaufgabe)	
2. Unterrichtsschritt: Charakterisierung von Cassius und Brutus	Schülervortrag / Unterrichtsgespräch	Cf. TA
3. Unterrichtsschritt: Brutus und Portia Text: II. 1. 234–303 II. 2. 8–56	Unterrichtsgespräch – Characterize the relationship between Brutus and Portia. – Characterize the relationship between Caesar and Calphurnia. – Compare the two relationships with respect to Brutus' character.	Brutus accepts Portia as an equal partner; she is strong and truly wants to share his inmost thoughts and problems in order to help him. Caesar is the dominant factor in this relationship. He uses with her the same arrogant style as he does in public. He sees Calphurnia as a typical woman whose moods and whims he at least respects for the time being. In his private life, Brutus is as frank and considerate as in his public life. In contrast to Caesar, he lives in real partnership with his wife.
4. Unterrichtsschritt: Brutus vs. Cassius	Unterrichtsgespräch – Which are the main differences between Brutus and Cassius?	Cf. TA
Hausaufgabe:	Read II. 1. 1–85 very carefully. Make sure you know the exact meaning(s) of every single word!	

© Ernst Klett Verlage GmbH u. Co. KG, Stuttgart 1988. Alle Rechte vorbehalten.

Tafelanschrieb:

Cassius and Brutus
(preliminary characterization)

	Cassius	Brutus
Attitude towards friends	scheming, manipulative (rhetorics, tricks)	considerate, frank
Attitude towards wife		considerate, loves his wife dearly and accepts her as an equal partner; Caesar in contrast: treats his wife as his inferior, but is ready to respect her female 'humours'
Attitude towards Caesar and a conspiracy	hates him as a private man because of his success and fears his political power; decided on action	loves him as a private man but fears his political power
Attitude towards Rome and other values / ideals	proud of Rome's glorious past; afraid of Rome's moral decline into tyranny	proud of Rome's glorious past; against a new tyranny; dedicated to honour and the general good
Judgements by other people	great observer and psychologist, at peace with himself, envious, very dangerous (Caesar)	loved by the people, high reputation (Casca); noble, but not without vanity; therefore open to manipulation by flattery (Cassius)
Summary	unscrupulous and selfish, successful schemer ←→	frank, honest, unselfish, and scrupulous idealist

© Ernst Klett Verlage GmbH u. Co. KG, Stuttgart 1988. Alle Rechte vorbehalten.

Beilage zu 925142, **Seite 18**

		Julius Caesar

11. Stunde:
Vorbereitung und Durchführung des Attentats

Unterrichtsschritte	Unterrichtsformen Fragestellungen / Impulse, Arbeitsaufträge	Erwartungen / Ergebnisse
1. Unterrichtsschritt: "oath" vs. "honesty" Text: II. 1. 86–140	**Unterrichtsgespräch / Kassette** – Explain the dramatic context and function of the meeting. Why does it take place in Brutus' house?	This meeting marks the "real" beginning of the conspiracy. The purpose of the meeting is to agree on the concrete execution of the conspiracy, especially on the following two questions: Should Cicero also be asked to participate? Is Antony to be spared? The meeting takes place in Brutus' house because Cassius wants to know Brutus' decision and because Brutus is the most respect member of the conspiracy.
	– Explain the difference between a "promise" and an "oath".	A promise constitutes personal obligation between individuals, whereas an oath constitues an obligation to laws or to gods.
	– Explain the contents and the structure of Brutus' address.	Cf. TA
	– Explain the functions of Brutus' address.	Cf. TA
	– Compare the recitation on the cassette with your interpretation of the address.	
2. Unterrichtsschritt: "sacrificers" vs. "butchers" Text: II. 1. 141–190	**Unterrichtsgespräch** – Who is the leader of the group?	Brutus is the leader.
	– Give three examples which show that Brutus is accepted as the leader by the others.	The others accept his decision in three cases: oath, Cicero, Antony.
	– Analyze and explain the imagery (structure, function) of Brutus' address.	One central antinomy of two images (sacrificers vs. butchers) which are further elaborated. The dichotomic structure of Brutus' address shows that he tries to hide before himself and the public the fact that he is going to commit a murder. Cf. TA
	– Comment on the argument about Antony's fate. Who is right?	Cf. TA

© Ernst Klett Verlage GmbH u. Co. KG, Stuttgart 1988. Alle Rechte vorbehalten.

Unterrichtsschritte	Unterrichtsformen Fragestellungen / Impulse, Arbeitsaufträge	Erwartungen / Ergebnisse
3. Unterrichtsschritt: Cäsars Ermordung Text: III. 1. 1–120	Unterrichtsgespräch – How is Caesar presented before his murder? Compare this presentation with the impression of his last words on you. – Describe the impact of Caesar's last words on our judgement of Brutus. – How is Caesar presented in the rest of the drama? – Describe the behaviour of the conspirators after the murder. Comment on Brutus' order to bathe their hands in Caesar's blood.	Caesar is presented as intolerably arrogant. His last words, though, show that he is also capable of deep human feelings like friendship and disappointment. We realize more clearly now that Brutus has betrayed his friendship with Caesar, which considerably questions his moral self-righteousness. From now on, we see Caesar only from the positive point of view of Antony. The conspirators believe that they have reached their aims (death of tyranny, liberty, freedom) and that they will be celebrated as the liberators of their country in the ages to come. Apart from that their reactions are rather confused. Brutus' order shows his original intention of making the murder of Caesar a kind of ritual sacrifice. To the spectator, though, it looks more like "butchery" than "sacrifice".
Hausaufgabe: Arbeitshilfe: Worksheet (für Hausaufgabe zur 12. Stunde)	Read III. 1. 124–274 carefully. Pay special attention to the question of how the figures are characterized by their behaviour and by other figures and whether these different points of view correspond with each other or not. Note down your results on the Worksheet.	

© Ernst Klett Verlage GmbH u. Co. KG, Stuttgart 1988. Alle Rechte vorbehalten.

Tafelanschrieb:

"oath" vs. "honesty"

"honesty"	"oath"
situation: – sufferings of their souls – tyranny ↓ strength of motivation: – to encourage cowards – to steel the weak spirits of women – we will fall for it ↓ aim / cause: – reforms – virtue of their enterprise ↓ promise: – honesty to honesty engaged – Romans that have spoken the word	 bad causes priests cowards souls that welcome wrongs

function: encouragement, pledge for high moral claims

"sacrificers" vs. "butchers"

"sacrificers"	"butchers"
want to destroy only the spirit	want to shed blood
cut only the head off	also hack the limbs off
carve him	hew him
act because it is necessary	act because they are envious
purgers	murderers

function: Brutus cannot really face the necessity of Caesar's murder.

Antony to be killed?

Brutus	Cassius
no	yes
people would not understand it	
Antony is not dangerous because he – will be a limb without a head – is given to diverse pleasures	Antony is dangerous because he – loves Caesar – is a shrewd contriver
wrong judgement → wrong decision because Brutus is an idealist with too many scruples	right judgement because Cassius is a realist without scruples

Presentation of Caesar

before the murder	last words	afterwards
intolerably self-conceited	very human	only positive (Antony's point of view)

© Ernst Klett Verlage GmbH u. Co. KG, Stuttgart 1988. Alle Rechte vorbehalten.

Unterrichtsschritte	Unterrichtsformen Fragestellungen / Impulse, Arbeitsaufträge	Erwartungen / Ergebnisse
1. Unterrichtsschritt: Die Bedeutung der Begegnung Text: III. 1. 124–274	Unterrichtsgespräch – Explain the importance of Brutus' meeting with Antony for the further development of the drama. – Explain the importance of Antony's monologue for the understanding of the meeting. – What are the main aims of the two opponents and in what other ways could they have acted?	Introduction of Brutus' antagonist, preparation of the turning point of the action in III. 2. In retrospect, Antony's friendliness is exposed as pure dissembling. Brutus: wants to win Antony as a friend or at least as a supporter of his reform. His options: not to meet Antony, to kill him during the meeting, not to let him speak at the funeral. Antony: wants to take revenge by rousing the plebeians by his funeral oration. His only alternative: to work secretly against Brutus.
2. Unterrichtsschritt: Brutus: „sacrificer" oder „butcher"? Text: III. 1. 165–173 Text: III. 1. 224–227	Schülervortrag / Unterrichtsgespräch – Explain Brutus' reactions to Antony. – Explain Brutus' statement: "I loved Caesar when I struck him". What does it tell us about Brutus' hierarchy of values? Whom would you prefer as a friend: Brutus or Antony? – Comment on lines 224–227: Is Brutus being cynical? – In his monologue, Antony calls the conspirators "butchers". Relate this statement to Brutus' speech to his fellow conspirators in II. 1. 162–183. Is Antony's accusation justified? Refer also to the actual setting of the dialogue.	Brutus naively believes that Antony will support him because he thinks he can explain satisfactorily why Caesar's death was necessary. Therefore, he receives Antony kindly and allows him to speak at the funeral. The statement is contradictory. It implies that for Brutus abstract values like the welfare of Rome are more important than private emotions like personal friendship. These lines show that Brutus not only believes that his deed was justified, but also that rational arguments can overthrow private emotions (friendship, love between father and son). Brutus wanted to be a "sacrificer", not a "butcher". This describes his altruistic intentions ("our hearts", 170). Antony judges from what he – and the spectator – sees ("the bleeding business") and from his personal love for Caesar. His view has its own logic.

© Ernst Klett Verlag GmbH u. Co. KG, Stuttgart 1988. Alle Rechte vorbehalten.

Unterrichtsschritte	Unterrichtsformen Fragestellungen / Impulse, Arbeitsaufträge	Erwartungen / Ergebnisse
3. Unterrichtsschritt: Caesar: „tyrant" oder „most noble man"?	Schülervortrag / Unterrichtsgespräch – Explain the portrait of Caesar hitherto depicted in the drama by Brutus and by Caesar's own behaviour. – Comment on Antony's positive opinion of Caesar in contrast to Brutus' negative eva-luation of Caesar: How are both judge-ments justified and what consequences has (or may have) Antony's position for the reader's judgement on Caesar? Refer also to II. 1. 10–34.	Cf. TA Antony's positive view of Caesar is founded on a strong emotional bias, on per-sonal conviction, not on any rational reasons. Brutus' judgement, on the other hand, relies on rational, though poor reasoning (cf. II. 1. 10–34). As the possible conclusions from Caesar's behaviour are also not really conclusive, the reader has either to make his own individual choice or to leave the question undecided.
4. Unterrichtsschritt: Antonius: ein ehrlicher Heuchler Text: II. 1. 165–189 III. 1. 144–147 und 231–236 III. 1. 255–274	Schülervortrag / Unterrichtsgespräch – How has Antony been depicted in the former parts of the drama? – Explain Antony's behaviour at the begin-ning of the meeting. – Explain Antony's address to the dead corpse in front of the conspirators. What can be deduced from it about Antony? Kassette / Unterrichtsgespräch – Evaluate Antony's monologue on moral grounds. What does the monologue tell us about Antony? – Try to find three criteria with respect to which Brutus and Antony are contrasting characters.	Contradictory. Cf. TA He masters the dangerous situation by skilful dissembling, without betraying his loyalty to Caesar. Overwhelmed by his sorrow and his emotions, Antony pats himself in a critical si-tuation. In contrast to Brutus, Antony is first of all Caesar's friend. Antony's thirst for revenge is understandable but irresponsible in its lack of moderation: Dominated by his strong emotions, he wilfully causes terrible suffer-ing for many people. Cf. TA
5. Unterrichtsschritt: Imagery of blood and destruction	Unterrichtsgespräch – Explain the dominating image in this scene. By what different means is its dramatic effect heightened? – What are the functions of this imagery of blood and destruction?	Cf. TA Cf. TA
Hausaufgabe:	Read III. 2. carefully. Write a short paper in which you describe the general structure of each speech by a few headings and short summaries of the respective parts.	

© Ernst Klett Verlag GmbH u. Co. KG, Stuttgart 1988. Alle Rechte vorbehalten.

Tafelanschrieb:

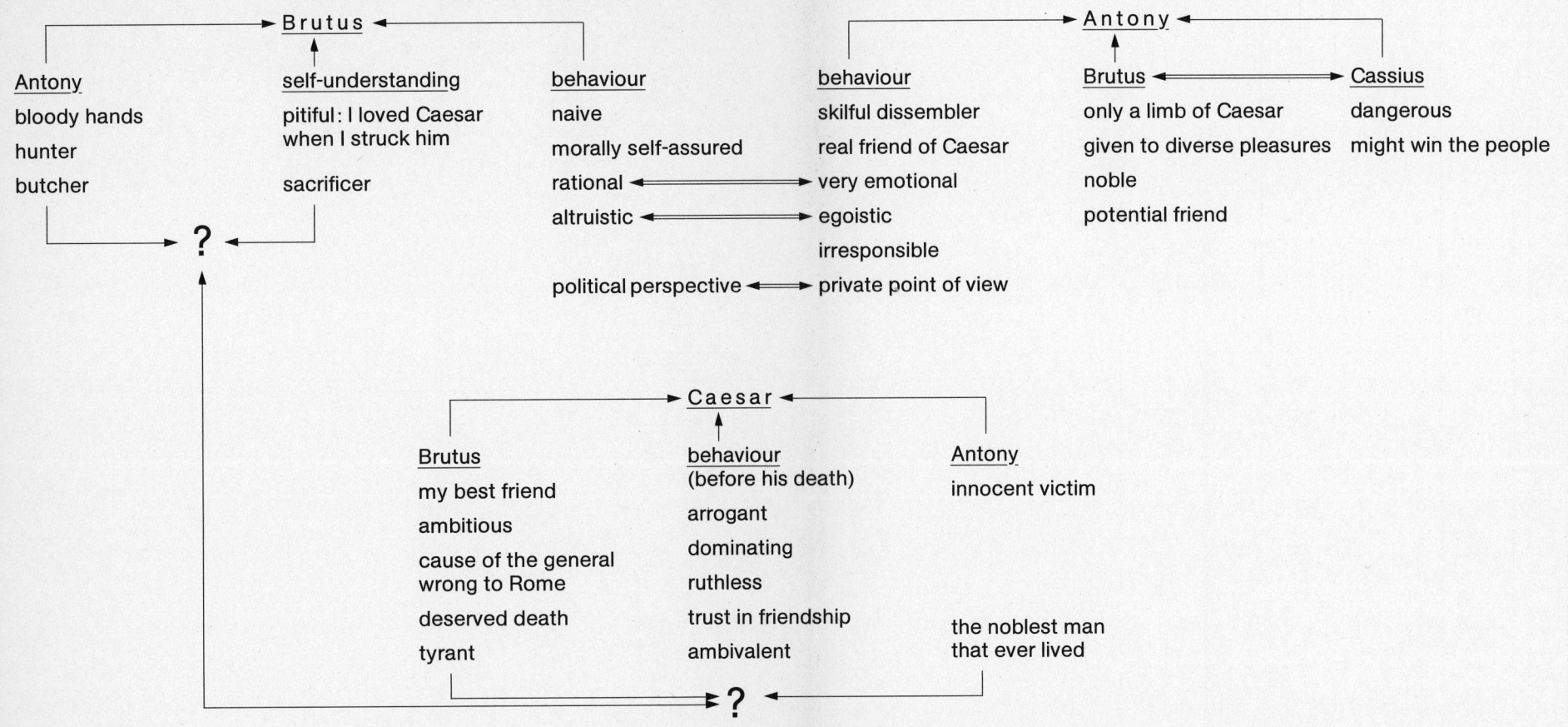

Brutus

Antony	self-understanding	behaviour
bloody hands	pitiful: I loved Caesar when I struck him	naive
hunter		morally self-assured
butcher	sacrificer	rational ⟷ very emotional
?		altruistic ⟷ egoistic
		irresponsible
		political perspective ⟷ private point of view

Antony

behaviour	Brutus	Cassius
skilful dissembler	only a limb of Caesar	dangerous
real friend of Caesar	given to diverse pleasures	might win the people
	noble	
	potential friend	

Caesar

Brutus	behaviour (before his death)	Antony
my best friend	arrogant	innocent victim
ambitious	dominating	
cause of the general wrong to Rome	ruthless	
deserved death	trust in friendship	the noblest man that ever lived
tyrant	ambivalent	
	?	

Imagery of blood and destruction

Objects: Caesar's bloody corpse, the conspirators besmeared with blood

Actions: Antony shakes the bloody hands of all conspirators

Language: "blood(y)" (10 times)
 Brutus: "bloody and cruel appearance" vs. "pitiful hearts"
 Antony: "hunters" – – "butchers"
  revenge: "blood and destruction" – – "havoc, war"

Functions

– sombre atmosphere = bad omen
– exposure of the repulsive reality of the murder = criticism of Brutus
– murder necessarily leads to revenge, i. e. more bloodshed and chaos

13. / 14. Stunde:
Techniken der Überredung II: Die Forumsreden

Unterrichtsschritte	Unterrichtsformen Fragestellungen / Impulse, Arbeitsaufträge	Erwartungen / Ergebnisse
1. Unterrichtsschritt: Brutus' Rede Text: III. 2. 13–63	Kassette / Schülervortrag Unterrichtsgespräch – Explain the structure of Brutus' speech. – Analyze Brutus' justification of the murder. What is Brutus' main problem here and why is Brutus' argument not very satisfactory? – Is Brutus' speech successful? – How does Brutus deal with potential opponents in his speech? – Comment on Brutus' use of language. – How does Brutus include the audience in his speech? – Give a general characterization of Brutus' speech.	 Cf. TA Brutus has to cope with the reproach of having killed a friend. His explanation that he valued the public good higher than his private bonds is very effective. But his argument against Caesar is weak in that he offers no evidence for Caesar's ambition. For the moment – yes. He disqualifies them as slaves and unpatriotic fellows which flatly contradicts hir former appeal to the wisdom of his audience. Prose, very formally constructed. Cf. the parallel sentence structures in lines 25–29. He really holds a monologue which ends in one question to the audience. Cf. TA
2. Unterrichtsschritt: Überblick über Antonius' Rede	Unterrichtsgespräch – Explain the structure of Antony's speech. Schülervortrag	Cf. TA
3. Unterrichtsschritt: Antonius' Gegenbeweise Text: III. 2. 75–109	Unterrichtsgespräch – Explain Antony's first reference (79–81) to Brutus' statement that Caesar was ambitious. – How does Antony try to cast doubt on Brutus and his statement? Analyze Antony's tactics in lines 87–103. – Explain the reactions of the audience to this part of Antony's speech.	Antony treats Brutus' statement as the hypothesis of a generally highly esteemed man. Antony gives several examples which show that Caesar was not ambitious. Each time he also stresses that Brutus is "an honourable man". Thus he tries not only to question whether Caesar was ambitious but also whether Brutus is really honourable. In contrast to Brutus, Antony has given them concrete evidence of Caesar's lack of ambition. Thus, he begins to win his audience. In addition, Antony ends this part with an effective emotional appeal.

© Ernst Klett Verlag GmbH u. Co. KG, Stuttgart 1988. Alle Rechte vorbehalten.

Unterrichtsschritte	Unterrichtsformen Fragestellungen / Impulse, Arbeitsaufträge	Erwartungen / Ergebnisse
4. Unterrichtsschritt: Indirektheit als Mittel zur emotionalen Beeinflussung Text: III. 2. 120–162	Unterrichtsgespräch – Explain Antony's rhetorical strategy in lines 120–129. – Comment on the use Antony makes of Caesar's will. – To what interests of his audience does Antony appeal with this part of his speech? How does the audience react?	By saying what he does not want to do, Antony shows his audience what could be done. At the same time he tries to create a split between the – honourable – conspirators on the one hand and himself and the audience on the other. Antony does not tell his audience the contents of the will, but how the common people and they themselves would react if they knew its contents. Cf. TA They condemn the conspirators as murderers.
5. Unterrichtsschritt: Antonius' direkter Angriff Text: III. 2. 171–211	Unterrichtsgespräch – Comment on the use Antony makes of Caesar's mantle and wounds. – Why does Antony concentrate on Brutus' stab in this scene? – Describe the reaction of the audience and compare it to their former reactions. How are these reactions connected? – Give a short sketch of the rest of Antony's speech. – Explain the use of the word "honourable" in Antony's speech. Kassette	The sight of the blood-stained mantle covering the corpse is shocking for the audience. It is apt to rouse deep disgust and hatred of the conspirators and strong compassion for the poor victim. Brutus' part in the murder is especially reprehensible because he has not only committed a murder but has also killed a good friend. The plebeians are almost besides themselves with rage. Three stages of reactions: 1. Acceptance of Antony 2. Condemnation of the conspirators ("murderers") 3. Call for punishment ("Revenge! Kill!") Again indirectly, Antony rouses the audience to open mutiny. Antony ends his speech with the proclamation of important items of Caesar's will. By the end, the plebeians have reached a state of destructive frenzy. At first, "honourable" is used in a purely descriptive sense, then with an invisible question mark, and in the end purely ironically.

© Ernst Klett Verlag GmbH u. Co. KG, Stuttgart 1988. Alle Rechte vorbehalten.

Unterrichtsschritte	Unterrichtsformen Fragestellungen / Impulse, Arbeitsaufträge	Erwartungen / Ergebnisse
6. Unterrichtsschritt: Vergleich der beiden Reden	Unterrichtsgespräch – Which are the main characteristics of Antony's speech? Arbeitsauftrag – Compare the two speeches as the expressions of two very different characters.	Cf. TA Brutus is a rationalist and idealist. He believes in the power of unadorned arguments and of his honour. Consequently, his speech is short, plain and sincere, and he shows no emotion about having killed his best friend. Brutus propagates abstract ideals like "Rome" and "freedom". Brutus is so certain of his success that he even leaves the scene before his potential opponent begins to speak. Antony, on the other hand, is cunning and emotional at the same time, and he knows that emotional appeals are more promising than cool arguments. His speech is concrete and full of images which appeal to the emotions of his audience. Antony propagates the material and emotional welfare of the individual.
7. Unterrichtsschritt: Konsequenzen Text: III. 3	Unterrichtsgespräch – Comment on 262/263. What do they tell us about Antony's character and intentions? Stille Lektüre / Unterrichtsgespräch – Explain this scene: Is Cinna really the victim of mistaken identity? – What are the consequences of the forum speeches for the future development of the action?	Antony is absolutely irresponsible. His sole aim is revenge at any price, i. e. the satisfaction of his private emotional needs. He does not mind what comes afterwards. It seems so at first. But the end of the scene shows that the plebeians, roused by Antony, are out to kill, no matter whom. Antony is the winner, not only of the rhetorical duel but also of the oncoming fight for power in Rome.
Hausaufgabe:	Skip through act IV so that you can summarize its contents. Prepare carefully the following passages with respect to the given questions: 1. IV. 1. 1–35 and IV. 3. 173–177: What do we learn about Antony and his party from these passages? 2. IV. 3. 1–28, 63–87, 93–118, 143–151, 200–228: Analyze this quarrel scene with respect to the previous characterization of these two figures. 3. IV. 3. 248–256, 278–289: What is the dramatic function of these two passages?	

© Ernst Klett Verlag GmbH u. Co. KG, Stuttgart 1988. Alle Rechte vorbehalten.

Tafelanschrieb:

Forum Speeches

Brutus	Antony

Intention: to explain the reasons for the murder

Intention: to rouse the people

Structure of speeches

Brutus

A) Introduction:
– reference to his honour
– appeal to rational and moral judgement

B) Justification of the murder:
Caesar, my best friend, was ambitious

C) Attack on possible opponents:
vile, unpatriotic people

Reaction of audience: "Let him be Caesar"

short / condensed
rational and well constructed
prose
plain
'monologue'

Antony

A) Introduction:
– reference to Brutus' honour
– reference to Brutus' assertion of Caesar's ambition

B) Rational means: positive evidence for Caesar
reaction of audience: Antony is noble

C) Manipulative manoeuvres:
1. appeal to material interests (Caesar's will) and emotions
   reaction: "They were murderers"
2. appeal to sentimental emotions
   (Caesar's wounds, Caesar loved Brutus)
   reaction: "Revenge! Kill!"
3. open appeal to mutiny
   reactions: "We'll mutiny"
4. appeal to material interests
   reaction: "Pluck down any thing"

long
emotional and seemingly spontaneous
verse / images
cunning
'dialogue'

Contrasts

Consequences

Antony wins the audience
chaos and civil war

"honourable"

Brutus =
honourable
honourable ?
a traitor !

+ → –

Caesar =
ambitious
ambitious ?
a "Caesar" !

– → +

© Ernst Klett Verlage GmbH u. Co. KG, Stuttgart 1988. Alle Rechte vorbehalten.

Beilage zu 925142, **Seite 30**

Unterrichtsschritte	Unterrichtsformen Fragestellungen / Impulse, Arbeitsaufträge	Erwartungen / Ergebnisse
1. Unterrichtsschritt: Antonius' Skrupellosigkeit Text: IV. 1. 1–35 und IV. 3. 173–177	Schülervortrag / Unterrichtsgespräch – Explain the meaning of these two passages. What do they tell us about the moral quality of Antony and his party? Give examples. – What characteristics of Antony have been displayed up to this scene and how do they relate to this scene?	Antony intends to cheat about Caesar's will and to exclude Lepidus from power over the Roman empire. In his evaluation of Lepidus, Antony displays an essentially inhuman attitude. The triumvirs have no scruples about killing close relatives and over a hundred senators. Cf. TA
2. Unterrichtsschritt: Die „quarrel-scene" Text: IV. 3. 1–28, 63–87, 93–118, 143–151, 200–228	Schülervortrag / Unterrichtsgespräch – Give a short summary of the quarrel between Brutus and Cassius. – What does Brutus accuse Cassius of? – Which deeper problem lies behind Brutus' accusations? Refer to Brutus' former appeal "Let's be sacrificers, but not butchers" (II. 1. 166). – How does Cassius defend himself? Try to devise a more effective defence for Cassius by explaining the implicit inconsequence of Brutus' argument in lines 67–75. – Compare Brutus and Cassius. – Describe the main phases of the development of the relationship between Brutus and Cassius. Pay special attention to the question of who is dominating whom at any one time.	Cassius feels wronged by Brutus because Brutus did not accept Cassius' defense of Lucius Pella. Brutus, in turn, reproaches Cassius of protecting corruption and thus betraying the moral principles of their conspiracy. The quarrel becomes more and more agitated, mainly on account of Brutus' intolerable arrogance. Cassius ends the quarrel by offering Brutus to stab himself which brings Brutus back to his senses. The two friends are reconciled. Protection of corruption, corruptibility, failure to send money for Brutus' troops. Brutus insists on the strict morality of their purpose _and_ of the means used to realize it. He is still dreaming of a clean and bloodless conspiracy. In II. 1, Brutus used the term "sacrifice" in order to persuade himself that Caesar's murder would not be a brutal act. Here, he tries to ignore the fact that wars include a certain amount of unjustice and moral muddle. Cassius could have pointed out that Brutus expects him to do the dirty work and chides him afterwards for it on top of everything. Therefore, Cassius could have accused Brutus of hypocrisy. Cf. TA Cf. TA

© Ernst Klett Verlage GmbH u. Co. KG, Stuttgart 1988. Alle Rechte vorbehalten.

Unterrichtsschritte	Unterrichtsformen Fragestellungen / Impulse, Arbeitsaufträge	Erwartungen / Ergebnisse
3. Unterrichtsschritt: Cäsars Geist Text: IV. 3. 248–256 und 278–289	Unterrichtsgespräch – What can we conclude from lines 248–256? – Discuss the reality of Caesar's ghost and its dramatic function.	Brutus is depressed and anxious, he wants to have company. A bad omen, signifying either that fate and circumstances are against the conspi- rators (= "real" ghost) or that Brutus has lost all hopes for a good ending (= ghost as a hallucination).
Hausaufgabe:	Skip through act V. Try to find out why the conspirators perish by reading the following passages carefully: V. 1. 72–119; V. 3. 23–96; V. 5. In addition, make a short list of wrong decisions made by Brutus previously and in act V.	

Tafelanschrieb:

The adversaries

Antony

lover of a gay life
skilful dissembler
very emotional person
real friend of Caesar
egotistic and irresponsible
great rhetorician
unscrupulous appetite for power

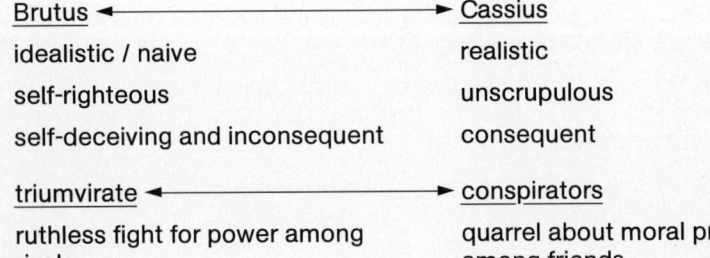

Brutus	Cassius
idealistic / naive	realistic
self-righteous	unscrupulous
self-deceiving and inconsequent	consequent

triumvirate	conspirators
ruthless fight for power among rivals	quarrel about moral principles among friends

Relationship Brutus – Cassius

Act / scene	Brutus		Cassius
I. 2	authority	——————▶	petitioner
I. 2. 310–323 / II. 1. 46–58	victim	◀——————	manipulator
II. 1. – IV. 3	boss	——————▶	underling
IV. 3. 107–124	friendship / equal standing		
IV. 3. 205–227	boss	——————▶	underling

("——————▶" = direction of influence)

© Ernst Klett Verlage GmbH u. Co. KG, Stuttgart 1988. Alle Rechte vorbehalten.

Unterrichtsschritte	Unterrichtsformen Fragestellungen / Impulse, Arbeitsaufträge	Erwartungen / Ergebnisse
1. Unterrichtsschritt: Brutus' Fehlentscheidungen	**Schülervortrag (Basis: Hausaufgabe) / Unterrichtsgespräch** – Give a brief description of wrong practical actions and decisions made by Brutus in the course of the drama.	**Tafelanschrieb:** R e a s o n s f o r d e f e a t I. Wrong practical actions and decisions – sparing of Antony (cf. II. 1. 154–185; cf. also V. 1. 45–47) – consent to Antony's forum speech (cf. III. 1. 233–244) – unsuccessful forum speech of Brutus – wrong military strategy (cf. IV. 3. 200–227; V. 1. 1–4) – Brutus' premature attack (V. 3. 5) Reasons – unrealistic idealism – faulty self-knowledge II. Resignation III. Fate
	– Explain briefly the different mistakes and try to find out what they have in common. – Explain the first three examples with respect to Brutus' character.	They were all mistakes of tactics resp. practical actions and were all made by Brutus (except his forum speech) against the explicit advice of Cassius. Unrealistic idealism: Brutus believes that such a good and moral cause as his will even convince potential opponents. Thus, he ignores the practical necessities of a revolution.
Text: IV. 3. 30–34, 51–60, 200–205	**Lektüre / Unterrichtsgespräch** – Read these short sections from the "quarrel scene" and explain them with respect to Brutus' military mistakes.	These passages show that Brutus is unaware of his practical or military incompetence: Brutus claims for himself not only high moral standards but also great military competence.

© Ernst Klett Verlage GmbH u. Co. KG, Stuttgart 1988. Alle Rechte vorbehalten.

Unterrichtsschritte	Unterrichtsformen Fragestellungen / Impulse, Arbeitsaufträge	Erwartungen / Ergebnisse
2. Unterrichtsschritt: Resignation oder Schicksal? (I) Text: V. 1. 72–92	Unterrichtsgespräch – Explain this passage with respect to the actual situation and Cassius' character. What does it tell us about Cassius' inner state?	Immediately before the battle, the pragmatic and active Cassius turns philosophical. He refers to his birthday, feels "compelled" to do battle, and explains a change in his philosophy. Cassius seems to have resigned, he apparently lacks confidence in their victory.
	– Comment on a possible relationship between Cassius' resignation and his new belief in omens.	There are two possible explanations for Cassius' lack of confidence: 1. Cassius tries to cover his understandable anxiety before the battle by referring to bad omens. 2. Cassius lacks confidence because of the bad omens.
93–119	– Comment critically on Brutus' philosophy.	Brutus' philosophy here is contradictory: At first he demands that people should patiently obey providence and the gods. But when he is faced with the possibility of public shame he values his honour higher than obedience to fate.
	– Summarize the parting of the two friends and explain its dramatic functions.	The fact that both conspirators only talk about failure shows their deep resignation. To the audience, this is a clear indication that they will die.
3. Unterrichtsschritt: Resignation oder Schicksal? (II) Text: V. 3. 20–25, 41–46, 63–71, 80–96	Lektüre / Unterrichtsgespräch – Why does Cassius kill himself?	1. Some of his troops have taken to flight. 2. Brutus' premature attack endangers their chances of winning. 3. Titinius seems to be captured.
	– Is Cassius doomed by fate or has he resigned too early?	Both explanations reinforce each other. Before Cassius has a definite result from Pindarus, he has already resigned and feels doomed. In consequence, he is all too ready to believe that Titinius has failed.
V. 5. 16–51	– Comment critically on Brutus' evaluation of his life.	Here, Brutus congratulates himself on his hounourable intentions, but ignores the hitherto and future sufferings of the people of Rome.
	– Explain Brutus' last words.	They may be understood as a last admission that his reasons for killing Caesar were not all that convincing even to himself.
4. Unterrichtsschritt: Epilog Text: V. 5. 68–75	Unterrichtsgespräch – Explain Antony's epilogue for Brutus and its function.	With Antony's epilogue, Brutus' "honour" is established beyond doubt. At the same time the other conspirators are criticized for mean motives. Antony speaks here more or less for the author.
Hausaufgabe:	Read carefully the following passages with respect to omens and their functions: Group A: I. 2. 1–25, I. 3. 1–78; Group B: II. 2. 1–90, III. 1. 1–12	

© Ernst Klett Verlage GmbH u. Co. KG, Stuttgart 1988. Alle Rechte vorbehalten.

17. Stunde: Vorausdeutungen und das Problem der menschlichen Freiheit		*Julius Caesar*
Unterrichtsschritte	**Unterrichtsformen** **Fragestellungen / Impulse, Arbeitsaufträge**	**Erwartungen / Ergebnisse**
1. Unterrichtsschritt: Hinführung	Unterrichtsgespräch – Let us collect some bad omens which people believe in. – What methods do you know by which people try to see into the future? – Which omens do you believe in? – Why are people superstitious? – What philosophical presuppositions do these superstitious practices have in common? – What consequences may follow from the belief in omens for the individual? – Why are people who believe in practices like fortune-telling called "superstitious"? Refer also to the German equivalent. – What is the main difference between Christian religions and superstition?	E. g. black cats crossing the street, broken mirrors, catastrophes, dreams E. g.: astrology, different techniques of fortune-telling (with cards, coffee-grounds, crystal balls etc.) They are afraid of the future and want to manipulate it. 1. Life is more or less predetermined, therefore it is possible to see into the future. 2. Nature is used by the gods or by fate to give man hints about the future, e. g. to warn him. He no longer decides for himself but is dependent on "hints" from the supernatural world; before taking decisions or actions he must ask his horoscope, fortune-tellers etc. . . . The term is used to separate "true" from "false" beliefs. In contrary to superstition in Christian religions, man is supposed to be free in his decisions and therefore responsible for them.

© Ernst Klett Verlage GmbH u. Co. KG, Stuttgart 1988. Alle Rechte vorbehalten.

Unterrichtsschritte	Unterrichtsformen Fragestellungen / Impulse, Arbeitsaufträge	Erwartungen / Ergebnisse
2. Unterrichtsschritt: Vorzeichen und ihre Problematisierung Texte: I. 2. 140–142, I. 3. 1–78, II. 2. 83–90	Schülervortrag / Unterrichtsgespräch – Give a brief summary of I. 3. 1–78. – How does Casca understand these strange events? – Comment on lines 28–30. – Describe Cicero's reaction. – How does Cassius react to the thunderstorm and Casca's interpretation of it? Refer to Cicero's sceptic remark. – Explain lines II. 2. 83–90 with respect to this scene. – Let us collect the possible meanings of the thunderstorm (those given in the text and others). – What are the dramatic functions of the thunderstorm with respect to the audience?	Casca, emotionally highly agitated, describes the violent thunderstorm and strange phenomena accompanying it at great length, first to Cicero, and then to Cassius. Either as an indication of a quarrel among the gods or as a godly warning and punishment for men's lack of religion. They show that people in Shakespeare's days tried to explain seemingly supernatural events in a rationalistic way as natural after all. Cicero admits that these events are strange but points out that all phenomena are open to human interpretation. Their "meaning" depends on the individual's point of view. Cassius almost derides the gods by walking around with an open jacket. Because he wants to win Casca for the conspiracy, he uses Casca's superstition for his own purposes and re-interprets the meaning of the omens: They are not a warning against impious behaviour but a warning against Caesar. Thus, Cassius exemplifies Cicero's statement. This is another example of the re-interpretation of an omen with a manipulative intention. Cf. TA The audience is to expect a gloomy and fatal action. Its second function is to create tension with respect to the question: Who will be the victim in the end?

© Ernst Klett Verlag GmbH u. Co. KG, Stuttgart 1988. Alle Rechte vorbehalten.

Unterrichtsschritte	Unterrichtsformen Fragestellungen / Impulse, Arbeitsaufträge	Erwartungen / Ergebnisse
3. Unterrichtsschritt: Die Iden des März	Unterrichtsgespräch – What omens relate to Caesar and what is their common meaning? – How does Caesar react to the omens in II. 2.?	Cf. TA He reacts in several different ways: 1. He orders sacrifices, i. e. he at least partly believes in their validity. 2. He believes stoically in fate ordained by the "mighty gods". 3. He questions that he alone is the object of the predictions. 4. He ignores the negative result of the sacrifices on account of his megalomania. 5. He changes his mind on account of Calphurnia's dreams. 6. He changes his mind again when Decius offers a flattering interpretation of the dreams.
	– Summarize Caesar's attitude to omens and explain his final decision to go to the capitol. – Explain the dramatic functions of the omens with respect to the meaning of the play and to the audience.	Caesar's attitude is ambiguous, wavering between respect and contempt of omens and superstition. The omens serve to stress Caesar's megalomania and his susceptibility to flattery. Thus, his death can be understood as a punishment for these two defects. Dramatic functions: creation of tension and / or prediction.
4. Unterrichtsschritt: Antonius' Fluch Text: III. 1. 255–274	Unterrichtsgespräch – What is a curse? – Comment on the meaning of these lines with respect to the given context in act III and as regards the end of the drama. – Relate the overall structure of the action to the two main omens.	A curse is a kind of magic practice, a kind of prediction which the victim cannot escape. In act III Antony's curse is mainly the expression of his love for Caesar and his uncontrolled rage at his murderers. Seen from the end of the play, Antony's monologue also acquires the quality of an effective curse and thus of a certain prediction or omen. The action of the drama consists of two distinct parts, i. e. the time before and after Caesar's death. Each of the two parts is dominated by an omen, the first by warnings about the ides of March, the second by Antony's curse. Cf. TA

© Ernst Klett Verlage GmbH u. Co. KG, Stuttgart 1988. Alle Rechte vorbehalten.

Unterrichtsschritte	Unterrichtsformen Fragestellungen / Impulse, Arbeitsaufträge	Erwartungen / Ergebnisse
5. Unterrichtsschritt: Zusammenfassung der erarbeiteten Ergebnisse	Diskussion – What dramatic functions do the omens have in JC? – Are the characters in JC free to act according to their own intentions or are they the helpless victims of their pre-ordained fates? – Explain the dramatic function of Antony's curse: Are the conspirators the helpless victims of some magic practice?	1. Characterization of persons by their reactions to and interpretation of omens. 2. Hints for the audience as to the future development of the action. 3. Creation of tension. 4. Authorial commentary. Cf. Notes on interpretation In some way they are victims of the curse, for the appearance of Caesar's ghost is a certain prediction in the drama. The curse and its destructive effects may be understood as a kind of "poetic justice", i. e. a critical authorial commentary on the conspiracy.
Hausaufgabe:	Collect arguments for "your" statement and against the other two statements. The statements are: 1. JC is a political tragedy. (group A) 2. JC is the tragedy of idealism. (group B) 3. JC is a drama of character. (group C)	

© Ernst Klett Verlage GmbH u. Co. KG, Stuttgart 1988. Alle Rechte vorbehalten.

© Ernst Klett Verlage GmbH u. Co. KG, Stuttgart 1988. Alle Rechte vorbehalten.

17. Stunde (Fortsetzung):
Vorausdeutungen und das Problem der menschlichen Freiheit

Julius Caesar

Tafelanschrieb:

O m e n s

The ambiguity of omens

example 'thunderstorm'

strife in heaven?

punishment for impious behaviour?

warning against Caesar?

warning to Caesar?

warning to conspirators?

natural phe-nomenon without meaning?

human projections?

Cf. Cicero: "men may construe things after their fashion, clean from the purpose of the things themselves" (I. 3. 34/35)

The ides of March

omens: soothsayer's warning
thunderstorm and other strange events
Calphurnia's dreams
warnings of the augurs

reasons: megalomania
susceptibility to flattery

reaction: Caesar goes to the capitol

effect: death

Ides of March → Caesar's death → Antony's curse → death of conspirators

Actions and omens

Dramatic functions of omens

characterization of persons
hints for the audience
creation of tension
authorial commentary